# WASHING THE STONES

## SELECTED POEMS 1975-1995

Other books by Maude Meehan
*Chipping Bone*
*Before the Snow*

# WASHING THE STONES

## SELECTED POEMS 1975–1995

*For Kath — Don't fall
far from the tree.
All good —*

*Maude Meehan*

Maude Meehan

Papier-Mache Press
Watsonville, CA

00 99 98 97 96 95   5 4 3 2 1

ISBN: 0-918949-85-8 Softcover

Cover art, "Inroads," © 1991 by Pat Mathews
Cover design by Cynthia Heier
Interior design by Leslie Austin
Composition by Erin Lebacqz and Leslie Austin
Author photograph by Ty Fairbank
Proofreading by Erin Lebacqz
Manufactured by Malloy Lithographing, Inc.

Grateful acknowledgment is made to the following publications which first published some of the material in this book:

*The Alchemist; Ally; Artemis; Coda; Community of Friends; Constellations; Coyote Bark; Demeter; El Andar; Egret; Green Fuse; The Holy Earth; In Celebration of the Muse; Kalliope; La Gazette; The Last Dance; The Limits of Miracles; Lighthouse Point; Lovers; Matrix; Moments in the Journey; The Moonjuice Anthologies (I through IV); Motherlife; Mother to Daughter, Daughter to Mother; Mothers for Peace; No More Masks; Pegasus Review; Poems from the Earth; Poems for a Livable Planet; Poetry Against Violence; Poetry of Place; Poets On:; Porter Gulch Review; Radar; Red Dirt; Sez; Sinister Wisdom; Somebody's Speaking My Language; Suicide Notes; The Tie That Binds; The Time of Our Lives; Touching Fire; Wild Duck Review; Women of the Fourteenth Moon; and Worlds Between Women.*

Certain words in this book reflect the author's preference for the British spelling.

Library of Congress Cataloging-in-Publication Data

Meehan, Maude.
        Washing the stones : selected poems 1975—1995 / Maude Meehan.
            p.    cm.
        ISBN 0-918949-85-8 (acid-free paper)
        I. title.
        PS3563.E295W37    1996
        811'.54.—dc20                                                      95-29997
                                                                                CIP

 *This book is printed on acid-free, recycled paper containing a minimum of 85 percent total recycled fiber with 15 percent postconsumer de-inked fiber.*

For my children
Donna, Christopher, and Charles
in memory of our *Ace*

# Acknowledgments

Special appreciation to Linda Bookout, Jerry Burke, Kathryn Chetkovitch, Greg Keith, Celine-Marie Pascale, Linda Selby, and to the women of my writing group, Lin Colavin, Amber Coverdale Sumrall, Candida Lawrence, Joan MacMillen, Dena Taylor, and Ellen Tree, for their invaluable support, and especially to Lillian Heritage.

# Contents

## The Cord Between Us: Mothers and Daughters

2    Mothers and Daughters
3    Connection
4    New Life
5    While There Is Time
7    Waiting
8    Lineage
9    Cartographer
10    Red Sky at Dawning
11    Album Circa 1912
12    Coda
13    Gift for My Mother's 90th Birthday
14    What Goes Around
15    Heritage
16    New Game Song
17    Letting Go
18    Turn and Turn About
19    To the Four Winds
20    Continuum

## Chipping Bone

## The Basket

23    The Basket
24    Child with Fan
25    Old Chinese Labour Camp
26    New Math
27    Guest Lecturer
28    For As Long As It Takes
29    Ritual
31    For a Small Dark Woman
33    No More Lowdown Blues
34    My Elder Sister, Newly Blind

35 Synapse in Summer Rain
36 Penumbra
37 Nursery
38 If Wishes Were Dancers
40 Sans Gloves
41 Escape
43 Inner-City Day Care Center
44 Chiaroscuro
45 Six A.M. Phone Call
46 After The Sixties
47 Peace Bridge to Canada 1969
49 For Kate, Somewhere in Nicaragua
51 El Barracuda
52 Nuclear Waste Plant
53 A Question of Time

Harbinger

56 Harbinger
58 What It Comes To
59 Crib
60 Small Son
61 Recompense for a Small Soul
62 Swift Wings
64 Graffito
65 Maxima Culpa
66 Father
67 This Dream
68 Dream of Winter
69 Reflections in an Old Mirror
70 Weight of Her Vision
71 Portrait
73 Women's Ward I and II
74 Women's Ward III
76 Echo of Sudden Silence

Out of Sync

78 Out of Sync
79 Summer
80 Reality and Illusion Tango
81 Son's Birth Day
82 Drum Talk

83    Fast Food
84    Overachiever
85    Gnawing Old Bait
86    Is There Life After Feminism

## Woman Tree

89    Woman Tree
91    Passage
92    Making Room
93    Interview
94    Pilgrimage
95    Litany of Alliance

# Before the Snow

## Genetics Revisited

99     Questions for My Grown Children
100    No Stranger at the Wedding
101    Semantics
102    A Sad Sweet Turning of the Tide
103    Early Lessons from the Maestro
104    Of Commission and Omission
105    Genetics Revisited
106    Kindergarten Report
107    Reclaiming Emily
108    Grave Site of a Small Son
109    Non-Birthday
110    Lament

## Groundswell

112    At the Embassy
114    Groundswell
116    Ernesto Interprets for His Mother
117    At the Book Fair in Nicaragua
118    Que Oscuras las Sombras de mi Sueño

## Answering the Question

120    Answering the Question
122    Questions When There Is No Note
123    Further Questions
124    Remembering Mary
125    Flight in Autumn

126   Bridge on 219
127   Suicide off Point Lobos
128   Limbo Again

## Before the Snow

130   Before the Snow
131   Corcoran Lagoon
132   Anniversary
133   Dahomey Woman
134   Harvest
135   Caveat
136   Mirror
137   Secret from a Large Lady
138   Behind the Walls
140   Trespass
141   We Are Not the Enemy
143   Howling Coyote Writes
144   The Shearing
145   The Great Escape
146   Explorers
147   Workshop
148   Kayla
149   Paean
150   The Passing

## Questions of War

152   Some Things Never Change
153   Questions of War
154   Documentary
156   Letter to Dennis
157   Letter from Sudan
158   Mollie's Restaurant
161   San Joaquin
163   San Joaquín
165   Prayer to the Ancestors
166   Why This Is Not a Poem

## Washing the Stones: For Acer

170   FOR ACER and all the years
172   Long Run Play

173   Response
174   List
175   Adventuress
176   Short Poem for Acer, Sleeping
177   Of Dreams, Nightmares, Osmosis
178   Fusion
179   Choice
180   On Second Thought
181   Greedy
182   Careful What You Wish For
183   First Things First
184   Ceremony
185   Companion of My Heart of My Life
186   Compañero de mi Corazon de mi Vida
187   In Time of War
189   Poem for Acer
191   Wrong Journey
192   For This Journey
193   Novitiate
194   Third Person Singular
195   death rattle
196   As the Thread Unravels
197   intruder
198   forewarning
199   Bête Noire
200   Aftermath
201   Kid Love
202   The Balance Game
203   Wharf to Wharf
204   Marking Your Absence
205   Rebirth
206   Treading New Water
207   Small Things
209   Imperfect Silence
210   Second Spring
211   The Other Side
213   Wishbones
214   Washing the Stones
215   A Chorus of Doves
217   Coin of This Realm

# WASHING THE STONES

## SELECTED POEMS 1975–1995

# The Cord Between Us

## Mothers and Daughters

# Mothers and Daughters

There is a cord between us
not yet cut
On it we move
like tightrope walkers
novices
uncertain of the net
Take tentative steps
across the gulf
toward one another
Careful
not wishing to turn back
Hopeful
that keeping balance
we can meet
can then embrace
and pass each other
as we must

# Connection

Across the continent
I feel your rhythm
pulsing in my veins.
The life you carry
sealed in fluid warmth
grows restless now,
prepares to leave
the center of your being.
I too grow restless
in my need to be with you,
my center waits your time.
My little calf, sweet daughter,
this mother, long removed
from young maternal care
is taken unaware
and overwhelmed by this fierce longing.

# New Life

My daughter's belly
moves beneath my hand
The child within her stirring
stirs in me a rush of awe
of mystery
so strong
so primal in its source
I touch infinity

# While There Is Time

I carry the folding chair
for my mother
I carry the shawl
the large straw hat
to shield her from the glare
She leans her small weight
on my arm    Frail legs unsteady
feet now cramped with pain

Each day we sit for hours
at the ocean    The sun is hot
but she is wrapped and swathed
her hands are icy cold
they hide their ache
beneath the blanket

Her eyes follow the
movement that surrounds us
the romp of children
flight of gulls
the strong young surfers
challenging the sea

When the visit is ended
when my mother leaves
I will burst from the house
run empty-handed to the beach
hold out my arms
and swoop like a bird
my hands will tag children
as I pass

I will run and run
until I fall
and weep
for the crushed feet
the gnarled fingers
for her longing
I will run for both of us

# Waiting

The nurse
marks an appointment.
It is my daughter's name
she writes.    Once more
the bow is drawn
the arrow aimed
at one of mine.
I wait for word.
The surgeon's verdict
finds its target
in my child;
it pierces me.
I cannot come to terms,
make peace with possibilities
that fracture reason.
I leave the house, go out
into the windswept day, bitter
to see the rainlashed trees
lose early blossoms.
Pacing the cliffs
I sense erosion
as wave on wave
sucks at the shore.

Along the far horizon, storm clouds
squat grey and swollen, waiting.

# Lineage

My mother
now grows old
Evokes the image
of her mother
now her twin

My daughter turns
speaks to her child
echoes my voice
and theirs
moves with our gestures
we are one
denying death
in this continuum

# Cartographer

I stroke her papery skin
now lined, worn tissue thin
as ancient maps
Trace with my aging hands
seamed furrows of my mother land
Explore the future

# Red Sky at Dawning

Together we go through your papers;
ninety-some years of garnering
old documents, certificates of marriage,
christenings, birth, and find an envelope
that holds a strange dry substance,
tissue thin, and neatly folded.
It is the caul that covered your small face
when you were born, like some sheer,
too prophetic bridal veil.

You say men of the sea were known to pay
great sums, that cauls were rare
and thought to bring good luck.
Then, with a rueful laugh remark
with luck like yours an admiral could drown
and all his shipmates with him.

Yet stories of your girlhood were like
fairy tales to me. Of how you tucked your hair
beneath your brother's baseball cap
and played all summer with a team of boys
who never guessed. Or of the longed for
Paris doll your older sister gave you
with its own trunk of hand-sewn clothes.
Stories of escapades with your exotic
cousins from abroad, and of your great
galumphing St. Bernard, the time you chased
the dog-pound wagon and retrieved him.

Tale after tale that made my childhood
pale beside your real adventures. Yet even now,
with all the hardships and regrets acknowledged,
knowing the love and the acclaim that came your way,
I count you fortunate as any seafarer
to weather proudly almost a century of storms at sea.

# Album Circa 1912

Mama
how beautiful you were.
Here you stand
beneath a sign
marked Danger,
laughing.
And this, my favorite,
where your rebellious hair
falls thick and soft
as summer heat
and promises.
Later the pensive
photographs emerge,
with pinned-back
hair and smile.
After illusions died
your eyes seem dark wells
of endurance.
The pictures blur
as stiff black edges
of the album crumble,
dressing my hands in mourning
as the pages turn.

# Coda

Our mother watches from her bed
as bureau drawers yield up the past.
A clutch of postcards collected over years
from places she has never traveled, never will.
Eight billfolds and as many purses for small change,
hairpins that fall from veils once worn to church,
small bits of jewelry saved for eventual repair.
Boxes on boxes holding gifts from loved ones;
scarves, gloves, tea towels, and hosiery,
all brand new,    too precious to discard.
How to divide?    She is so anxious to be fair
wanting her children each to share these treasures.

Days later, when the long familiar rooms
are echo empty, we wheel her
to the ambulance that waits. She gives
no backward glance, but sits, so small
yet somehow regal, and clasps the armrests
hoping to hide from us the tremor of her hands.

# Gift for My Mother's 90th Birthday
*Burcham Hospital*

We watched the rain sluice down
against the window of your sterile room
and listened as you told of childhood's
summer showers at the farm; how you ran out
a colt unpenned, into their sudden soaking bliss.

Now you, aged changeling mother,
emptied and clean as a cracked china cup
on the wrong shelf, whisper, "What I would give
to feel that rain pelt hard against my face."

But you had nothing left, so we
conspirators of love locked the white door
and your granddaughter wheeled you to the bath
where we unclothed your little sack of bones
and lifted you beneath the shower.

She held you up, your legs pale stalks adangle
and clasped your wasted body, bracing her taut
young flesh to your slack folds.
And you clung laughing, joyous as a child
to feel the clear fresh rivulets
course down your upturned face.

# What Goes Around
*for my daughter*

The day I brought her home
you came without my asking, and
with patient, practiced, nurse's hands
lifted your grandmother
as though she were a child,
explaining carefully
how I must raise her up, just so,
how to attend the angry seam
of her incision.
And I recall with sudden tender rush
the day I brought you home,
my newborn daughter, firstborn child.
Reminded now, how she whose helplessness
rests in your arms, took you
with loving care from my unskilled
young hands. Taught me to bathe you,
how to bind the scarlet stem of cord
cut sharply at your birth.
Here in this room, invisible, yet strong
I sense our lifelines joined,    and pulsing still.

# Heritage

Mother
how frail you are,
bent like a question mark.
The answer in your eyes.
White hair, milkweed down,
I blow and wish on it,
my wish denied.

I watch as you slowly
drift from us,
slowly let go.
Pure essence remains,
your life force, love.
Old one, dear one,
you will not leave us empty.

# New Game Song

Propped in a chair
there sits a pale lady
quavery white haired
wisp of a lady
who made up the games
I played as a child

She has disguised
the strong hands
that held me
gnarled them like ginger root
knotted with pain

See how she plays now
pretends not to know me
pretends she's forgotten
even my name

Mother
please tell me
the rules of this game

# Letting Go

Life and your fast approaching death
have stripped you of all passion,
all possessions, all amenities.
Even the desiccated husk
that houses pain and pride and gallant courage
fades and daily shrinks before my eyes.

Against translucent skin, white hair
gone thin as cobwebs clings
to your delineated skull, and I can see
the waning thread of blood move slowly
through a blue transparency of veins.

Crooning our old loved lulla-bye-bye song
I gather up your crumpled frailty.
Daughter to mother, hold you, rock you outward
toward the tranquil, longed-for place.

# Turn and Turn About

The phone call comes,
the one I've been expecting, but
is always unexpected. Acer holds me,
pulling a rueful face
remarks we are both orphans now,
two seventy-year-old orphans.

That night, in bed
we laugh again at the absurdity.
I laugh and laugh and cannot stop
and suddenly am five years old
and lost, and just as suddenly
the hot tears come and come.

# To the Four Winds

*for my mother, Ethel Barrett, 1889–1987*

Your children
    grandchildren
    great-grandchildren
    gather

The gone-befores
    are here with us
    in our memory
    in our keeping

We hold fast
    to all you taught us
    what we learned
    from your living

We give you back now
    to the earth
    to the sky
    wind and water

Small crumbled
    bits of bone
    soft grey ash
    silence

We bury sorrow
    sing you outward
    fly with you
    hearts open

You are the seedpod
    in its bursting
    replenishing
    the earth

# Continuum

Almost a year has passed
since you let go of life.
Spring comes.
Outside the window
small migrant birds
move delicate as grace notes
on the wire. I watch a sparrow
pull dead twigs from the porch vine
to weave into its nest below the eaves.
A daughter's belly swells,
a grandchild moves toward life,
and you are present for me
in this promise, in these affirmations.

# Chipping Bone

---

*I want strong peace,*
*and delight,*
*the wild good.*

*—Muriel Rukeyser*

# The Basket

# The Basket

long past ready for opening
hinges rusted
clasp broken

the fakir's flute mislaid
perhaps hidden

the uncoiling dreaded

the trapped heart
scurrying behind ribcage

pulse squeaking
*not yet    not yet*

the fear alive

the basket
empty

# Child with Fan

Fragile as the fan you hold
folding    unfolding
ivory ribs
The bird appearing
disappearing
on painted silk

Your breath held

Your skin ivory silk
hair burnished feathers
Small careful fingers
delicate
hollow bones of bird

I watch you unfolding
My breath held

# Old Chinese Labour Camp

*Nisene Marks Redwood Forest*

*The songs of small caged birds*
*were heard behind walled gardens*
*in the province of Khuan Ye*
*Blown on salt breeze the scent*
*of incense moved through early*
*stunted pines, mingled with prayers*
*for sons' and husbands' safe return*

Only harsh warning cries of nesting birds
break eerie silence on the mountain trail.
Through failing shafts of light
chill wind stirs fingers through the vines
that creep to cover remnants of a camp
where alien men once lived.
Thick odor of decay hangs over roofs and walls
of shacks collapsed against tall trees.
Close by a ledge of rock reveals, unlikely,
out of time and place, a trace of fossil shells
faint etchings of fish vertebrae
cast by upheaval of an ancient sea.
Strange hieroglyphs on unfamiliar land
where moss and scales of lichen
draw their blankets over quietly.

# New Math

"Two halves comprise a whole"

Einstein and Lobachevsky
those geniuses
who spun
refined and cosmic
distillations
mathematically confirmed
this simple fact

Yet I cannot accept it

My morning orange
cut in two
loses sweet juice
upon the board
And this    this ball
once sliced in half
however neatly glued
will never bounce again

Too lately made aware
I sense in things divided
even things mundane
the cauterized
fine line of scar
the stain
invisible to those
well armed with logic

# Guest Lecturer

With patronizing politesse
you first dissected then dismissed
the works of Sexton, Plath, and Lorde,
using such adjectives as self-indulgent,
neurotic, and of course, confessional.

I bought a volume of your verse,
finding them etched on dazzling cerebral snow
with icicles that would not melt or pierce
or dare to shatter in your hand.

I searched that tundra's vast expanse
in quest of spoor, a drop of blood,
a burst of wings. And finding none
turned back to that exquisite heat
which glows so perilously close to flame.

# For As Long As It Takes

I remember your face
before webs fretted its surface,
holding old dreams.

A time when clock hands met
applauding all your midnights
and each day opened bright
with promise that you kept.

Now nights crawl by,
dawns heave the weight
of morning news, all bad,
against your mind's closed door.

You hide behind its guarded pain.
I reach to draw you out.
Old friend, I remember your face,
love even your shadow.

# Ritual

Wasted lady
takes the scarf
she will wear
for her lover

Ties it tightly
around her arm
he is her knight
it is his pennant

The silver spoon
and the candle
are made ready
in his honour

She prepares
to receive him
lights the flame
melts the powder

She exists
for this moment
counts the hours
till their meeting

How subtle
his seduction
how willing
her surrender

In the hollow
of her arms
he embroiders
threads of scarlet

Seeds of death
surging through her
seal their union
bind her closer

Satisfied
she unwinds
silken folds
wraps him slyly

Safely hidden
he lies waiting
in the coffin
of her room

# For a Small Dark Woman
# in a Small Dark Place

Slat skinny in that flashy dress,
face raddled as Georgia mud in winter,
you had us crazy for you
at that wall-to-wall jammed concert
three, or was it four long years ago?
You took us high, then higher,
hotter than any fantasy,
then cooled us, hushed us into tears,
singing with all the pain and fear
that ever sprung from being black
and filled with woman knowledge.

This morning, driving the freeway
flipping the FM dial,
your wail hooked out and caught me.
And I thought about that nightclub
where I saw you only weeks ago.
No twelve-piece band this time,
no strobe-lit platform,
and no cheering fans. You showed up late
and moved onstage somewhere between
a stagger and a stumble, and midway through
you spaced out on the lyrics.
The backup trio covered up
like it was nothing new. Playing for time
you threw an apathetic bump and grind
and heard the snickers turn to catcalls.

For what seemed like forever you stood there
dazed, and stared out blinking
at an audience gone silent.
The bass man tried to lead you off
but you turned and brayed a scream
that sent your pain right through me.
And I held it, when what I wanted
was to hold and comfort you.
But that would only have stepped harder
on your pride, so I just slipped out
real quiet, and drove home and yes, I cried
remembering that other time.

How you stood hands on hips and sassy-ass,
feet planted wide, laughing and bragging,
"Ain't *nooobody* gonna bump their uglies
on this sister less she say so."
And how we all laughed raucous with you,
loved you, proud, with just a piece of jealous
thinking you had it all together, wrapped and tied.

*Died August 17, 1984*
*Esther Phillips, age 48*

# No More Lowdown Blues

Who can forget
the way they whispered
wailed and sung,
those women hung on meat hooks
in men's minds.   Who can forget
the names of Marilyn and Janis,
Lady Day;   how they fulfilled
all fantasies, all expectations
but their own.   Too vulnerable,
too frail, their masks of toughness
membrane thin, they sat
strung out,   worn out,   alone.   Stared
into late night, early morning mirrors.
Saw booze and needles, bruised tired
"tits 'n ass." Saw end to hope,
and chose an end to dreams.

Now we must sing for all our sleeping sisters,
used tired women everywhere.
Not lullabies or lowdown blues,
we have new woman dreams to share.

# My Elder Sister, Newly Blind

Strapped in the belly of the plane
I sit, eyes tightly closed
behind dark glasses.   Experiment, in an
attempt to understand what it must mean
to live trapped in the endless night
that is my sister's sightless world.
Wonder if my face like hers, wears the strained
look of listening with nerve ends.
I fumble with the seat belt, grope
for the sweater that I drop.   Flinch
as a body presses by to occupy the seat beside me.

Later the beverage cart clinks down the aisle.
My neighbor's disembodied voice, Midwestern,
jovial and deep, requests a double scotch.
Prodded by curiosity and ennui I glance across
and see the casual ease with which he pays,
reminded how she fumbled in her bag.   She says,
*"It isn't hard. I use one paper clip for singles,*
*two clips to mark the fives. I never carry much.*
*Counting loose change by touch is easy, once you learn."*

Eyes closed again, and bored for what seems
an eternity, I cheat and check my watch, find
only half an hour has passed.   Give up pretense,
devour my book and feast my eyes on sunset till we land.
I seek my husband's face among the waiting crowd,
not ready yet to speak of darkness, or how my sister stood,
smiling, head high and shoulders back,
and waved good-bye to me,   facing the wrong direction.

# Synapse in Summer Rain

Rain thrums against the window
where someone large has wheeled her.
Wet leaves cling to the glass,
limp as the shawl the old woman draws into.
Her fingers pick and pluck and worry
at its fringe. Questions have become puzzles,
answers forgotten, along with her name
and the faces of strangers who are her children.
She peers out at the rain.    Effort ripples
the still pond of her face.    Wait!
Something flashes, silver slippery as fish.
*A girl running    To someone?    From someone?*
Her brow furrows,    *Yes, a girl running swiftly*
*light as air,    as rain,    in a wide green place.*

# Penumbra

Ancient, brittle as thin December air
she has been tucked and wheeled
like some unseemly infant
to sit before a noisy flickering screen.
Slivers of light shutter the bony
death mask of her face; eyes closed,
deaf to all voices that talk at her
and past her, she nods in and out of sleep.
What she chooses to see and hear
held safe, within the quiet of her skull.

# Nursery

The first cramp
grips her
she waits
is certain there is time
before the birth
then feels the clench
of sudden second cramp
a gush of water
bursting
drenching legs—
reaches to wake him
encounters empty space

Awakes confused
to rows of beds
sees crumpled forms
the creased
cloned faces
of outworn
old women
like herself
who pee and mess
their diapered thighs
through seamless
nights and days
merged hazy
tranquilized

# If Wishes Were Dancers

It was about Magic
the closing of eyes
the wishing

>    nothing impossible
>    a small girl's size
>    her size

Not the unreal or real of it
only the wishing

>    for sequins and spotlights
>    her silver toe-taps flying
>    eliciting *Ohs!* and *Ahs!*
>    and again *Ohs!*

And the mirror wishes

>    for golden tresses
>    long silken strands
>    Rapunzel hair

Dark frizzy mop ignored
clumsy sneakers not considered
Cross cluckings of disapproval
unheeded   unheard

the scant ration of wishes granted
overlooked

>    the real of it
>    in the possibilities
>    in the believing

Grown now    Grown-up now
Grey middle-aged confusion
muddled by residue
rituals outgrown

the nagging voices louder
listened to

and her feet    her feet mired in wishes
her eyes still closed

# Sans Gloves

I thought them ugly once
now with new vision see
my hands, these strong
good friends as beautiful.
No longer hiding in my lap
they go in public naked
and they dance for me.

# Escape

Here is a room held like a globe in summer heat
blinds drawn against the aching eye of sun
A room bathed in subaqueous half light
where only flash of fish behind curved glass
moves soundlessly suggesting life

Picture the woman in this room who sinks
in humid sleep    This woman dreams
she too swims iridescent    sweeps waving
frond of fin    long fan of tail

> *only her gentle gliding*
> *only her gentle gliding*
> *only her graceful gliding*
> *is real    is real    is real*

Distorted mouths emerge in air
blurred through the waters of her dream
Voices cause waves to crash against her ear
strident they call her name

Watch as she rises slowly    slowly
moves on reluctant passive feet
to tend these gaping mouths
that chew and speak    unspeakable
these dream destroyers    blindly unaware

> *her hands    only her hands*
> *feed these piranhas of her life*
> *only her hands are theirs*

Picture once more this woman as night falls
as she retreats from life    embraces sleep
closed in the airless sultry room
weighted with hate and heat    See now
the curtains as they move in the first breeze
sway in the first cool quenching wind of night

Do not look further    No one can see her
as she answers    stirs sinuous and spiny
in the dark    Sheds luminescent fin and fan
for wings that arc and carry her
to soar and wheel    This woman answers
            from her dream

> *only this graceful gliding*
> *only this graceful gliding*
> *only this silent secret flight*
> *is real    is real    is real*

# Inner-City Day Care Center

Late afternoon
bone tired
mothers straggle in
Corinna
swaggers through
her strut a signal
that she seethes

The others
pick up on her cue
slip into jive talk
to confuse
and bug
the tightass
social worker
whose distaste
is written
on her whitefish face

Hey it's an old hype
the fastest one in town
flashing the style
from shufflefoot
to ghetto hip
No points    no score
and no way any winners
in the game

Behind dark hands
shrill laughter
stifles pain

# Chiaroscuro

Tony
Sequined drag queen
Small sepia perfection
Begging rejection
Setting me up
Say Black
Say Gay
Send me away

Tony
Wears cynic's eyes
Kaleidoscopes
Of mock obeisance
To centuries of lies
Pours from his cup
Fermented anger
Laced with longing

Tony
Streetwise hip hustler
Holds my child
Caresses corn silk head
White starfish hands
Explore dark skin
Black cloud of hair

Their eyes
Their worlds
Collide
Meet soft as air
Each one reflecting
Accepting
Only innocence

# Six A.M. Phone Call

Your voice rips sleep away,
disintegrates
three thousand miles
six months
of false reprieve.

Hand tense on the receiver
I will myself not to receive
the hunger in your voice.
Force myself to recall
friends, lovers,
family you left.
Returning now and then
to feast on us and leave.

Your travels now
are circumscribed,
from cell to ward
to street and back again.
Only your counselor remains
and you complain she feeds you
Thorazine instead of words.
I cannot nourish you,
I know that now.
This cupboard's stripped
of all but pain.

You're right; there's no one left,
no, nothing more to say.
The vacant hum of wire swallows you
as you did us, with mindless
impervious detachment. Aching
I place the phone back gently
in its cradle. Lost man,
I cannot do the same for you.

# After The Sixties

The decade that shattered us
is already a myth
Battle sites blur on folded maps
faded as names of martyrs
on old newsprint

The young turn from folklore
legends that do not concern them
Faint memory of tear gas
hangs in polluted air
silent as past echoes of gunshot
and the still mouths of dead children

The oppressors wield staffs
pretend to be shepherds
The sheep mill in concrete labyrinths
their lambs gazing on AstroTurf
of quiet campus lawns     The herd
sucks at the swollen breast of media
bellies bloated with delusion

The avenging angels who roamed the land
long-haired and barefoot
truth howling from their lips
and their eyes bleeding innocence
have disappeared     All but a handful
labouring over poems and pamphlets few will read

I shuffle the used cards of my fear and anger
reading them over and over for a sign
Nothing appears     They shuffle like worn
slippers of old men     warriors     wandering
aimless and impotent seeking their lost dream

# Peace Bridge to Canada 1969

The underground is organized
takes only calculated risks.
Still, I am always apprehensive.
A pale young woman
slides into the car.
She is composed and cool,
we do not speak.

We stop, next passenger,
Army deserter, young,
nervous, neatly dressed.
We run an ID check
on one another,
rehearse new names,
drive on in silence.

We have our orders,
follow the set rules.
Exchange no information,
no careless word,
no clue to true identity.
Know it is possible
that one of us
could be a decoy.

The border guards
wait at the bridge.
I roll the window down, smile,
wonder if paranoia smells.
We are questioned, waved on,
our facade accepted.
Innocuous sightseers,
mother, daughter, boyfriend
bound for Niagara Falls.

Miles pass, quiet, tense
we watch for the sign,
Toronto City Limits.
Arrive at last
at the appointed place.
He leaves the car,
we pull away.
Return without incident,
part without words or touch.

I reach my home,
say that my day was spent in shops.
Tend to the dinner, embroider,
read a book. Then wish
Goodnight, rest well,
to my young sons who sleep
in warm familiar rooms.
Turn on TV for news of war,
hear the box score
of maimed and dead.
Silent, subtract by one, and go to bed.

# For Kate, Somewhere in Nicaragua

You travel inland on the backs of trucks
jammed in with chickens, goats
old women huddled under shawls
and ancient silent men, and always,
always without warning, the roadblocks,
the unpredictability
and arrogance of Contras.

By now there are small bits of information
you will have gathered,
some useful for survival
and some not. By now you will know
all that you will ever want to know
about the cold metallic sweat of fear,
the gaseous smell of death,
the dance of maggots in the sockets
and how the staring eyes are first to go.

Between the world you move in
where the dispossessed and dead still multiply,
between that world and here
where we wait anxiously,
news travels slowly.   The wires
are crossed with lies
told by the ones whose cocks swell
at the smell of money,
and whose hearts are wallets.

I have this dream,
you stumble toward thick jungle,
dense silence broken by your ragged gasps
and from the bundle that you carry
a high, thin wail.    Last night
the dream again.    This time you stopped
and turned, arms empty,    darkly stained.
I ran to help you, but you disappeared.

Today I dredge for prayers
that women have offered up for centuries,
but fear still sits like some stale sacrament
upon my tongue.    I travel with you
and your child into that void
where prayers and loved ones vanish without trace.

# El Barracuda

*Santa Rita Jail, June 1983*
*Anti-Nuclear Protest*

On those nights when a certain guard
paces back and forth, back and forth
in the tent where the women are held,
the air is thickly silent.
If the rattle of his keys ceases, suddenly,
close by a cot,   hearts lurch,   heads
turtle down under stiff blankets,
the feral odor is that of fear.
In the grey dawn as we stumble to the toilets
he watches,   thick fingers stroking his truncheon,
the teeth of his smile large and white.
The pale flat eyes follow our buttocks,
leave trails of sperm on our breasts.

# Nuclear Waste Plant

*Buttermilk Creek, West Valley, NY*

Across the creek
a steel mesh fence
stretches for miles
to guard the monolith

The grass
is bleached
along the bank
There are no sounds
save the swift rush
of water over stone
the drone of flies
who swarm to shroud
a stiffened bird

Beyond the fence
a cautious doe
nudges her fawn
down the steep
slope of creek

All awkward grace
on straddled legs
it bends to drink

# A Question of Time

*for Rachel Carson who warned us*

It has been said we do not pass time, time passes us.
We are aware that it grows late.

The winged creatures and the animals,
the roe of the sleek fish, all these are tainted.

Poison seeps into our children's bones
from the milk of cows grazing in lush fields
and the air, the soil, the water, are no longer safe.

It is understood that we are lied to.
That for long years these things were kept from us,
learned only by accident or mistake.

In clear tidal pools anemones draw soft fronds
into tight buds as the crab scuttles close.
But how does a woman swollen with child flee the
great metal insect spraying the air she breathes?

We are angered by avarice and deception.
The copper taste of insecticide is not so bitter
as anger that grows rancid when we do not act.

We are told there are levels of mercury,
of nitrate,    of radiation,    that are *acceptable,*
that in war there *acceptable* casualty rates.
That to prevent war we must deprive the people
to add to the stockpiles for our genocide.

We must relinquish the illusion of safety,
form a shield for the old and the innocent,
the helpless ones.   Cry out
in our rage, in our passion for life,
*"None* of these are *acceptable."*

The time is upon us, almost past.
We cannot waste it or the earth will be laid waste.
Only the hot wind sifting thick grey ash.
Only the wind keening.

# Harbinger

# Harbinger

death's visits are untimely
more frequent

he seeks out my loved ones

burrows into their luggage
crawls into pockets or purses

as they pack for journeys

lately he is visible
it is a secret
                that passes between us

i glimpse him in depots
                               airports
fingering their tickets

his hand
waves next to their hands
                as they leave

i wave back
my smile a rictus of terror
                as they disappear

when they are distant
he thrusts stained garments
                into my dreaming

i rend them
bind their past sweetness
                in my hair

tangled and matted
snarled in dark ribbons
                i awaken

burn joss sticks    refuse messages

# What It Comes To

Sorting what's left is mawkish business;
you'd be the first to scoff at sentiment.
I'm trying to make sense, but it's too soon.
Or else too late.

How many years I stood aside and watched you
at your easel.   Admired your stained
and lizard-quick lean hands and loathed
the smell of turpentine at war with gin.

Watched as you thrashed upstream
against the current, only to land
outraged in shallow waters, when
what you wanted was the open sea.

Even in youth you were the cynic,
short on compassion, and your
sardonic mouth kissed and cursed life
with equal fervor and drank of it, unmindful.

Now in harsh light beside the open window
the fevered purple tongues of iris lick night air,
clawing their unslaked roots into the earth;
parched earth I can't believe you lie at peace in.

# Crib

It is too silent here

Small as a toy
you lie so still

Your puzzled frown is fixed
and empty

My breasts fill
not knowing they weep

Not knowing I cannot wake you

# Small Son

They have gone
the last mourners
the last comfort
last cliché

I wrap a pillow
in your blanket
lie burying my face
to hold your fading
milk-sweet smell

The silence swells

      I run

to where the stand
of saplings
waits for clearing

Chopping    slashing
small limbs
piled for burning

Only a pall
of smoke arises
this tender growth
too green

# Recompense for a Small Soul

Your grave opens over and over

You move between your brothers
the dark one and the fair

the ball tossed
no eyes catching its movement

Mine see the arched spine    the arm drawn back
never your face

I am cheated of the least knowledge
of what your life might have been

Yet all around me there is cheating
boxed voices droning lies

evil smearing its fecal hand over eyes
stopping mouths

It is then that I see you
spared

All painful possibilities erased
with your brief life

When even the man who runs the corner store
smiles as he thumbs the scale

I count my change with care    Hoard
what is left to me

# Swift Wings

She has withdrawn from us.
A small mound blurs
the angled line of bed.
A woman,    older than her years
lies waiting for release,
her worn face carved
from early softness
into scraps of wire and flesh.

Unused to rest, her hands
lie quiet on the spread;
their veins reveal
a pulse each hour more secret.
At last flow falters,
ebbs beyond our tracing.

The vigil ends.    Footsteps
descend the stairs, dislodge
white powder from a ceiling crack.
It sifts through sunlight,
drifts, and settles on a cat
caught in an eye of light.

Neighbors arrive.    Set covered
dishes on the table
where hired hands had nattered
over crops and cows and endless meals.
Then one by one approach the man
who sits, a weathered bull past prime.
Speak in hushed voices of a woman
they assumed they knew, who ran
a treadmill to and from that board.

Retreating to the sink, I slosh
wet busy work.   Clutch at her clumsy
bar of homemade soap, and see
her lye-scarred hands as I had
come upon them once at early dawn,
kneading great lumps of dough.
Naming each yeasty rising mound
his name,   and pounding, pounding.

Or once,   when as a child I watched
unnoticed as she trussed
a turkey for his pious Sabbath meal,
saw her become a sudden fury
flailing tense fists
against its unresponsive flesh.

Before me on the narrow sill
her meager plants bend toward the light.
A movement in the window calls my eyes.
The rooster struts,   trails from his spurs
a slime of unborn life and broken shell.
Above,   against the morning sky a sharp
calligraphy of small swift wings take flight.

# Graffito

I find a snapshot in my father's drawer,
a picture of the grandfather I never knew.
Small, stooped yet dignified, he stands
beside my brother's wicker pram
surrounded by his family.
My mother tells the story, hidden in the past,
of the last time she saw him. Tells me
that she was big with child, and so allowed to sit
while his two daughters served the sons
who gathered at the table.
Grandmother reigned as always at the head;
arranged the seating of those sons
not in the order of their age
but of the weekly wage they earned
and without question brought to her.

I learn that you, mild gentle man
never at home in the new language, the new land,
subdued by failure, each passing year withdrew
further into old world memories and silence.
Rising that evening from the table, as usual
scarcely noticed as you went to lie down on
your narrow bed, there was no sign, no signal.

Only that as you passed, you bent with shy
and unaccustomed show of tenderness, to murmur
"Liebchen," and kissed my mother's head.
She tells me that I leaped and struggled in her womb
when from your room you shattered silence with a shot.
Your life exploding messages across blank walls in bursts of red.

# Maxima Culpa

On Cayman Island the old fisherman told you
that after the turtle is caught
and hacked from its shell the flesh squirms
steaming on the deck

"Thees mon seen them pieces jump all night.
Sometime they still jumpin' next day."

He won't eat turtle    the spirit is trapped
"Bad juju."

Last night you were with death again
No real embrace    A moist flick of
your tongue between her lips
to let her know you're still interested
Not ready to settle down but willing to gamble
No needles this time
Downers    booze    the desperate phone calls

And next time maybe there won't be anyone at home
Out of town    happy hour    the movies
who knows where    and no time left    Maybe
you try one last number    but a machine answers
and you panic    "For Christ's sake *listen to me!*"

Maybe next time we'll find your shell
stiff and empty    And we who love you
stripped raw    quivering    trapped in your pain

# Father

Frayed remnants
will not weave
into a fabric
I can handle
Lay out
in all its length
to make a garment
Six years now
since your death
and still no pattern

# This Dream

A murky broth
stirred
with long twisted spoon
I dip my fingers
draw careful
crimson flowers on my breasts
The petals dry
brown brittle edges curl
become old photographs
I will not recognize
Pale
tremulous young brides
dust veiled
whose eyes
pick nervously at silence
Music begins
a dissonance
a needle rasping
in worn grooves
Sharp tinny voices
scold me to dance
Stricken
on crooked legs
I cannot move
This dream
has chipped the bone
at its most fragile joining

# Dream of Winter

Trees hedge the darkness
      where I skirt the edges
            of remembered pond
Test with sharp silver point of skate
          prod at the pale bland face of ice

*What is it you are waiting for?*

and I glide swift to center
         deaf to the hingey creak
            and crack of warning
as I spin and twirl
      whirl faster as blades hiss
            "thin ice   thin ice"

*What is it you are waiting for?*

Ice opens

Answers from a cold dark eye

# Reflections in an Old Mirror

Mirror,   I held you
in childish innocence, in ignorance,
searching the don't touch place.
Seeking the hidden wound
that spattered red across your face.

Mirror,   I turned away confused and shy
in my virginity and caught your stare
reflecting him.   Framing his grace
as he knelt over me, wiping my blood
from his warm cock.

Mirror,   I watched my baby born.
Watched in your glaring ceiling eye
the reddened skull, bulging and thrusting
from my strapped spreading thighs.
My son burst forth in spurts of blood,
in sudden crimson beauty.

Mirror,   I held you to my baby's lips.
Begged that you steam and blur
with infant breath.
Your cold clear face reflected his,
a tiny pinched blue mask
stained with dark blood.

Mirror,   though I shatter you in dreams
I cannot destroy what you have shown me.
I am bled dry as the sound of your splinters
cracking under my feet.
Even in dreams afraid to look down,
see my reflection
shattered in my own blood.

# Weight of Her Vision

*Prisms of light*
    *pierce*

*Small grafts*
    *itch*

*Scar tissue*
    *draws*

*The tic relentless*

# Portrait

I.  Wearing the face
    of habit
    by day
    she moves serene
    licks down
    the ruffled fur

    In sleep
    she mewls
    blind suckling
    seeks the empty tit
    curls naked
    mother to herself

II. Island
    in an ocean
    of amniotic fluid
    a wash of cells
    red as the faces
    of her past newborns
    as they yowled
    for sustenance

    Receiver
    of nightmares
    from outgrown beds
    she hears
    the cries of hunger

III. Medusa
   skull crowned
   with writhing umbilici
   Severed
   her pulsing sensors
   still bleed
   still bind

# Women's Ward I and II

I.  Mantis

Waiting
fragile legs
drawn in
antennae
drawn in
wings folded
still as death
To be a stick
a twig
pretending not to be
hoping to escape
the hungry mouth

II.  Isolation

Alone
wears no disguise
alone
is absolute
in that abyss
Mind emptied
spirit bleached
under
relentless glare
only cocoon
of skin and hair
remain

# Women's Ward III

*Ne Pas Déranger*


Do not disturb
the door is closed
there is a sign
on my silence

Words are mercury
they are silver
they are liquid
I cannot capture

Here is my skull's
bony basket
in its hollow
wool lies softly

It is unspun
it is uncarded
nothing weaves
or is woven

In my sockets
are definitions
articulations
they do not translate

My eyelids
are transparent
I lie gazing
without vision

In my distance
sheep are grazing
they absorb
all my colours

The world is white
it is muffled
there are no ears
there is silence

Fleece is snow
snow is crystal
if I speak
it may shatter

There is a sign
on my silence
it is foreign
it does not translate

# Echo of Sudden Silence

A darkened stairwell
And the razored scream
Of falling
You rag-dolled at the base
Long slender column
Of your neck askew
The shocked O
Of your silenced mouth
A dark stain pouring

# Out of Sync

# Out of Sync

my neighbor is orderly as an alphabet
her footsteps are predictable
familiar with maps and signposts
without her there would be pandemonium

screened from her sight by the nicotiana bush
I succumb to its swoony smell
hummingbirds' beaks dart into its blossoms

the unflappable lady peers over the railing
Discovered!   my sticky chin and fake wings

# Summer

Apricots ripen
Plump monks
Sunning
In saffron robes

# Reality and Illusion Tango

They have forgotten their old language
speak fluent cliché.

He wears boredom like a bruise and sinks
behind a poultice of newspaper.
Her mouth wears reproachful stitches;
she can't find herself in his mirror

Arguments drone,    a worn cassette
they play over and over.    The tape
is a serpent's tongue,    darting
into cracks that grow wider

Evenings limp into nights
the pillows have lost their feathers
bedsprings rusted.    No rumpled sheets

# Son's Birth Day

Squalling
crumpled face outraged
a tiny frog
thrust
from his tadpole refuge
unleashed a stream of pee
Statement
against life's first indignity

# Drum Talk

Next door
each day
all day
you play
reggae
blues
country western
hot top forty
at top volume
The heavy beat
of bass
thumps
through thin walls

Each night
all night
the slightly
turned down
blanket
of your music
slides
inside my dreams
and sends them
winding
reel to reel

Tomorrow
I'm buying
bongos

# Fast Food

His charm
like his sincerity
donned carefully
for the occasion
was, how shall I put it,
not a veil, though
suddenly transparent.
More of a winding sheet
for expectations
or cloth for
the anticipated banquet
where he spread
stale offerings.
Did he think, oh
did he really think
she was that hungry?

Closing the door
she snuffed the candles
ignored the empty table
and her belly's growl.

# Overachiever

Enough of textbooks for tonight
Studies of cybernetics pale
beside the cosmic revelations
to be found in skin on skin
Come love, forget your grades
to fail this moment's promise
is the greater sin

# Gnawing Old Bait

Ah brain
you convoluted mouse
accept
what's done is done
Regret is futile
*the trap's already sprung*

# Is There Life after Feminism
*(or, how to wear boots and still be politically incorrect)*

I like to wear boots.
I like the noise they make.
I walk real uppity in boots.
I walk strong.
If pressed
I can land a punch, a kick,
demolish a rapist,
and if I want to
I can go to bed in boots.

I cook without tofu or eggplant
and I hate alfalfa sprouts. Call it heresy.
I hug my husband, my sons,
and send my daughter radical feminist literature.
I hug her too.   I hug my gay friends,
and don't apologize for being straight.
I hug my friends of colour
and won't apologize for being white.
How can we stand up together
if we're putting each other down?

I am a senior citizen.
There are advantages.
I get ten percent off on pancakes at Golden West
and a dollar off at the Nickelodeon.
Sometimes I wear lipstick, mascara
and don't ask anyone's pardon.
I wear a dress when I visit my mother.
She's ninety-six; I'm sixty-five.
Spare me your arguments.   Where is it written
that any one of us has all the right answers
for anyone else?

I am a good citizen.
There are *dis*advantages.
I write to presidents and politicians,
and they do what they want anyway.
I go to marches, to meetings, to jail,
and I have a file in Washington in my very own name
which I refuse to send for.
I know who I am.
Even when I do dishes, mind kids or wear heels
I know who I am.
But what I like about wearing boots is,
there's no confusion.
*Everyone* knows who I am.    Watch out!

# Woman Tree

# Woman Tree

I have lived
over half a century

The rings of my growth
have been recorded

Record this also

The embrace of my roots
is fierce

The earth
yields to them

Yields to my growing

My taproot reaches down
through dark ages

I am nourished
by ancient springs

My least twig

Knows the strength
of my branches

My fruit
is bittersweet

I bloom

Again and again
with my own rhythm

I defy the seasons

# Passage

It is an old friend
an old enemy
    this knowing
it is time
for the next journey

I look longingly behind
    the gate is closed
I am eager    yet
peer cautiously ahead

The shadow I carry
slants away from me
    I stumble
it leans forward
    pulling me on

Locked in this quest
    we press
toward an elusive noon
the moment
    of merging
in clear white light

# Making Room

My workroom walls
Ragwrap collage
Clutter of clippings
Collision course
Death and destruction
Political explosion
Sudden implosion
Signals
Signposts
To clarity

What moved me
Why I am here
Claiming
Room

# Interview

You ask how I think others see me,
you ask how do I see myself.
Could you be more explicit,
pinpoint in which surroundings
and at what hour of the day or night.
You see coworkers find me organized
unlike homemakers in whose eyes
I seem somewhat haphazard.
Conservatives see a flaming left-wing type
and yet it's true that radicals deplore
my bleeding heart, my knee-jerk liberal view.
To those whose lives are dissolute
I seem a pillar of stability
while those more stable disagree.
My mother sees me still her little girl,
grandchildren find me venerably aged.
My husband views the face of lover-wife,
our children drown in chicken broth
as I breaststroke through each life.
It seems the single me you seek
within the maze, the crazy Fun House
of life's fair, seldom stops long enough
to stare into the Room of Mirrors and to wonder
where distortion meets reality—
and if she really knows, or cares.

# Pilgrimage

I see a landscape of women
Some wander from group to group
seeking leaders
Many are mute    Though all
know the language of signs
There are stretchers
to carry the crippled
over rough new land
No maps exist
but direction is clear
Mountains loom on the horizon
shrouded in mist
only the valleys are familiar
They press forward
gaining momentum
as their numbers increase
Seismographs record tremors
of unknown origin
Needles tremble and radar
shows gathering storm
There are rumors
reports of apprehension
in fortresses and high places
I see a landscape of women arriving
surging    singing    scaling the walls

# Litany of Alliance

Every woman who knows

that she has been patronized
    or trivialized

Every woman who has been called weak
      called neurotic
      called hysterical

*and who among you has not been named*

Every woman whose aging
      has rendered her invisible
or by her youth or age
      has been seen as powerless

Every woman who has known poverty
      who has watched
      her children's eyes grow dull
      who has heard the sound
of their bellies growling

Every woman who has been stunned
      by the weight
      of her own revelation

Look to *all* women
      to the old for their wisdom
      to the young for their daring

Turn to your sisters
      whose skin is
      the colour of honey
      the colour of earth
      the colour of almonds

Look into their lives
    and weep for their knowledge
    make a bridge of your sharing

Joining together we come to our power
Joining together new strength is born

# Before the Snow

*I would meet you in that open space*
*at the center where the real words pulse,*
*where the meaning is.*

—*Irene McKinney*
Six O'Clock Mine Report

# Genetics Revisited

# Questions for My Grown Children

Is it a burden that I ache along with you,
share not just your joy, but pain?
And do you know how much I want to be
all that you wish, and yet how much
I sometimes balk at expectations,
real or unfounded, and imagine
that the same holds true for you?

Does it make you uneasy to be so loved,
and does it sometimes comfort you?
It is the only love without condition
I have ever known or given.
And in your middle age, my old,
can you be patient with me, and accept it,
and can we keep the closeness we have shared?

# No Stranger at the Wedding

We have not seen you
since you were a child
son of our brother
who died far too young.
Now you have flown
through twenty years,
three thousand miles
to join the gathered clan
who miss his light.
Waiting for you we reminisce,
recall his wit
as pointed as a dancer's toe,
speak of his grace of spirit, then
grow quiet in our longing
for what fades from memory.
But you arrive, wearing
his high-domed lozenge of a face,
speak with the sweet deep timbre
of his voice, greet us
with a remembered smile
and bring your double gift to this reunion.

# Semantics

You said my sons were drifting
Times proved you wrong you know
Fearful, you saw them drift
Joyful, I watched them flow

# A Sad Sweet Turning of the Tide

My two young sons
move with assurance
through the maze
of ropes and sails,
steer out of turbulence
to calmer seas,
drop anchor.

They climb the mast,
my body tenses
with past apprehension.
Suddenly one dives.
I plummet with him,
breathe again
when he emerges.

The small boat pitches
as he hoists aboard.
I glance up swiftly
to the swaying crossbeam
where his brother perches
confident, secure.

A heavy mist rolls in.
They guide the light craft
safely back to harbor
and like my hands,
old maps lie folded in my lap.

Reaching the laddered dock
they stretch strong arms to steady me.
When did this turnabout occur?
I have become a passenger
on their journey.

# Early Lessons from the Maestro

My father taught me early on
to love the flow of language,
the music that it made.
But such sad tunes he played,
songs, poems or stories
rife with improbable catastrophes.
Tales of small children orphaned,
their parents lost at sea,
or star-crossed lovers, doomed.
And he, when I would inevitably cry, smiled
with benign approval, satisfied.
Oh, I was Daddy's sensitive "good girl"
too young to recognize, to know,
that Mother played second fiddle in our trio
and he used subtler means to bend the bow.

# Of Commission and Omission

My Father, who may be in heaven
I write this in your name.

My Father, who said I could do anything,
be anything, because I was like him.
Who wanted my loyalty, my attention,
my love,   undivided,   unconditional.

My Father, who out of his own need
patronized his sons,
who was jealous of his sons,
who used my childhood
to diminish my mother.

My Father, who died a bitter man
because he was no longer rich,
no longer young, because he was unheralded,
unsung, by a world that would not
recognize his genius, self-proclaimed.

My Father, who may be in heaven,
I am only beginning to understand
what daemons drove you, what shaped you,
and why ambivalence is acid-etched
across this portrait, blurred
by victim blaming victim, the twisted
convolutions spiraling in our wake.

My Father, whom I loved, whom I still love,
forgive me this trespass, as I have forgiven
you your trespasses,   in the name of my Mother,
your Sons,   and of your Restless Ghost.

# Genetics Revisited

How heady the sweet freedom of summer on the farm,
our father hard at work in the hot city
not there to dampen us with admonitions
against drowning, snakebite, every possible disaster;

our small adventures, secret laddered climbs
to hide up in the haymow all the sweeter
knowing he would have scolded us to earth,
his fledglings not supposed to fly.

Long years have passed and he is truly gone,
victim of nothing but time's passage. And I
who swore her children would remain unfettered,
watch them, and all the children of the world, and worry.

It isn't my affair, but I am troubled
by that small boy playing near the curb,
cars whizzing by as if he were invisible,
or by that girl hitching a ride at
the next corner in a car that pulls away
before I have a good look at the license or the driver.

I know it isn't any of my business, but those strands
of DNA grow stronger, and I who tempted perilous fate
and drove my father to despair, can hear him laughing
somewhere in the distance, and I worry.

# Kindergarten Report

Beware, square peg,
there is a file
on you already.
Let me quote,
"This child believes
that flowers are alive,
should not be cut.
This child insists
that he and animals converse."
The list goes on,
proves beyond doubt
you are perverse.
And what is worse,
they'll change all that.

# Reclaiming Emily

I still have dreams of you,
skinned rabbit of a girl, fist sized
and otherworldly, born too soon.
See you curled glistening
in that steel basin, the cord
that should have nourished you,
a tentacle about your throat.

Brusque and indifferent, the nurse
whisked you away as if you never had existed.
No one addressed the aching loss
except to say that there was time,
there would be other children,
or worse,    turned from me with that silence
that holds question,    blame.
So I,    alone and young in time of war
and easily intimidated, did not name you,
even to myself. Your brief longed for
existence christened only by my tears.

Now long years later, I stand in ritual circle
with strong women, acknowledging the powerful
constant in our lives. Each speaks her mother's
name, her grandmother's, her daughter's,
and once again that small sharp jab
against my heart, demanding recognition.
Here in this woman circle, at last
I speak your name aloud, and claim you.

# Grave Site of a Small Son

You still rise in dreams,    return
in the scent of grandchildren,
their soft skin, their cries.

You are buried in my heart.
No lid to close.
How can I forget you?
Who else will keep you alive
remembering your sweetness?

While I live you will know how I loved you.
When I die, I will take you with me.

There will be only these poems.

# Non-Birthday

Today there were no candles and no songs,
no festive dinner with family gathered round.
Long years have passed since you were here
bright, beautiful and strong, but tears
like memories, rise in me all day long
and I have not forgotten.

# Lament

Little one    Little one
why are you resting
pale in the dark
when the children I watch
at play in the park
are rosy and warm and round

Little one    Little one
deaf as a stone
to the wind in the leaves
and the bright birds' song
what are you doing
down in the dark
under that mossy mound

Little one    Little one
lying alone
shrunken so small
and dry as a bone
me here above
left to rock and to moan
and you so deep in the ground

# Groundswell

# At the Embassy

*Managua, Nicaragua*

Below the terrace frayed leaves of the banana trees
rustle in rising wind. Red-winged *chocoya*
dart from branches with shrill cries
as a dark wall of rain appears on the horizon.
The changing light takes on a purity,
an incandescence that defines white blossoms
of the *sacuanjoché* with the vividness of colour.
Lush is the word that curls my tongue
until the wife of an ambassador, a small, gaunt woman
with an indefinable accent, speaks,
her thin voice slicing air as paper slices skin.

She mentions that they were once stationed in Bombay,
tells us the monsoon season there, unfortunately
resembles this. "Yes," she continues, "one grows
so tired of inferior posts, same heavy humid air,
same drenching rains and mud, rank smells,
the wizened children with old eyes,    at first
so guilty making, but one soon grows used to them."

And she goes on,    her rasping breath the sound
of something tearing,    to speak of her weak lungs,
her heart,    and for her captive audience
examines with a jeweler's loupe
a host of early aspirations,    unfulfilled.

Sags with regret made palpable, then adds,
"Forgive me, I am tiresome, but as you see
I take too long to die, a joke life plays on one
perhaps exacted for old sins. Truly it robs one
of any saving element of tragedy. Don't smile,
I am reduced to boring new arrivals like yourselves."

Rejoining us, her husband shrugs with exaggerated
patience, interrupts. "We were speaking of small,
underdeveloped countries were we not?
Amazing, isn't it, how cleverly the weak wield power?"
Silence descends, as weighted as the steamy air;
as if on cue the downpour closes in.
Grateful, we scatter like the *chocoya* to take cover.

# Groundswell

*Nicaragua 1985*

Bombs and a great earthquake have toppled
the handful of high buildings in Managua
to the ground. Only the Bank of America
now looms, its phallic spire jutting
from the rubble. We pick our way out
through the roofless shell of the cathedral
where scrawny cattle forage among rocks
and glass and stiff dry knots of stubble.

I stumble, Mauricio steadies me, warns gently,
"Careful Señora, some stones they dance in earth,"
then asks, "Last night did you see on the television
the henchmen of Somoza, and did you mark
the princely stone that winked from the Colero's ring?
We saw it as he hung his arm like a long snake
around the shoulders of your presidenté."

My daughter wept and cursed him,
saying it glittered like the hunger in the eyes
of her small children. "Mi amiga, there is much
we cannot understand. Your country fought
as we have to be free, yet they conspire
with our oppressors to control this land."

Again I stumble, and again he steadies me, and speaks.

"Here we believe that some stones still remember
how they fell to earth, trailing a blaze of fire
in their flight, and so at night they dance, hoping
to keep from being trapped forever in hard earth.

Often when we were small, our mother would point
to the dark sky and say, *See there,     the ones that wink
at you, those are the brave and stubborn who persisted
till the wind took pity, and she raised them
that they might light the way for others in the night."*

I looked to where he pointed in the darkness, and I swear
there was a stirring in the ground around my feet.

# Ernesto Interprets for His Mother

*Esteli, Nicaragua, 1987*

You tell us that you are but a small fish
in your big country, but like us you swim
where sharks infest the waters, and like us
you learn that those who wear the teeth of sharks
devour even the smallest in their way.

I have already lost two sons, a daughter,
and a grandson to the struggle, and who knows
where, or whether they are buried. I only know
my joy was buried when they disappeared.

Thanks be to the Virgin, Ernesto who was wounded
can stay here to help me farm. Between us we care now
for my daughter's children, but I am tired, and I tell you
anger leaps always in my belly like an unborn child.

You have walked openly among us, you have seen
that we are free to worship as we please,
that campesinos now may farm their land.
Now all may learn to read and write
and women walk the darkened streets in safety.

And yet the hope that fed our hearts no longer fills us.
We fear there is no chance your leaders
will cease to arm the Contras, or that the cruel embargo
will be lifted. They point the guns of hunger
at our bellies that they might bring us to our knees.

Ernesto hesitates, then adds, "My mother does not mean
to speak with impoliteness. It is most kind of you
to come to us. We only wish that you go back
to tell your people what is true, and who it is
that feeds them lies. Señora, pray for us.
May God go with you that you make a safe return."

# At the Book Fair in Nicaragua

Ortega strolls among the people.
Cardenal, the priest-poet, walks with him,
a good target, and near him a tall man
whose face is gentle, vice presidenté
of this small, beleaguered country;
a writer of books and poems
whose life has been threatened.

Beside them is Ortega's brother,
the one who escaped,
the only brother who is left,
his fingers immovable, curled
like the lotus, lily of death
by bullets spit by Contras.

They move freely through throngs of people
without soldiers or Secret Service.
The multitudes part before them
smiling, calling out. I think of Moses,
the Red Sea parting, and how simple,
how blind, how beautiful is faith.

# Que Oscuras las Sombras de mi Sueño

*How Dark the Shadows of My Dream*

Small scarlet birds, swift signals of danger
scatter, become bright splashes of blood
on the worn pavement of cathedral steps.
I grope in darkness through ruins of the city.

Lean-boned children surround me, bring me rice.
A thin grey cat snakes at my ankles
waiting for kernels to drop. I cannot eat.
The little ones stand in the shadows, watching,
hold out their hands, palms up, murmuring softly.
I cannot hear what they say, but I sense what they ask.

Suddenly smoke spews from the volcano Santiago.
I flee from its warning through an empty landscape,
my feet bogged in ashes. A fleshless horse stands
unyielding, unprotected, under torrential rain.

I am rescued by a wagon with tin plates for
armor, there is no driver, yet I am taken to the fair.
It is La Piñata, and music gives way to the voice
of the poet-priest whose words bless the air.
I learn what it is that starves these children,
this verdant land. I know now who it is.

I stand at the edge of the crowd, stare into the
spellbound eyes of campesinos. They will not turn,
or be turned away. The night shudders with longing,
I try to speak but my tongue has no language.

The world stirs outside my window. I awaken
as thin northern light pervades my room,
remembering your molten sun, Nicaragua, your beauty,
your courage, haunted by dark shadows of my dream.

# Answering the Question

# Answering the Question

Did I ever tell you
of the dead opossum
wedged in a crawl space
underneath the house?
For weeks it filled the place
with that rank sick-sweet smell
that permeates your pores
and coats your skin.

And when you ask me
why I seem preoccupied
with death, I only know
it's what spills out
when I sit down to write
of all those things
that make me love life
with an ache that beggars
explanation; and then
the sea mist drifts in
through the open window
wraithlike in the night
and curls around the lamp
as though alive and lost,
demanding to be recognized
if only in the these words.

Once you have placed the phone
back on its hook, refusing
to believe that there will be
no final word or touch, or look;

when death stares back at you
out of the eyes of someone
dearly loved; once that has
happened, it waits all around you
in simple unexpected things
that wince the heart.

A scent that rises
from a seldom opened drawer,
a note in a familiar hand
scrawled in the margin of a book.
Even the repetitious click
made by a child's stick
dragged along a fence,
echoing the sound that lid makes
when it closes down, and locks.

When death grows too familiar
it seems closer than your skin,
and in the midst of laughter
on the brightest days
whispers to you of hubris,
the air around you suddenly thick
with a familiar sick-sweet smell.

# Questions When There Is No Note

*for Amy at 19*

The white coat diagnosed post-adolescent
angst, not true depression, and ordered up
a quick fix, try this, try that mix
of brightly coloured jelly beans
whose magic blurred all jagged edges,
quickened slow pulse, or made the reels
run backward to a better time.

In your grey, separate space, they seemed
like minor miracles. Quick, luminous epiphanies
that for a brief while banished emptiness,
in place of family, of friends, of love.

But then, you loved yourself to death
in mirrors where you razored down white lines
and needles spun you out and out,
then further out, on threads already frayed.

No one could reach you in that chosen distance,
but still we wonder, were you gambling
the way kids do, thinking they too are magic
and immortal; a macabre joke that backfired?
Or was it desperation, past any comfort
or our comprehension? Still we question.
Question, as if any answer could assuage the pain.

# Further Questions

Why must I lose each one of you
again and again? Why does
remembrance refuse you your rest?

You busy yourselves in my dreams,
never a day older than when you left,
all of you whispering reminders
into the curve of this ear,
allowing me glimpses
as you turn a corner,
enter a strange door,
disappear.

When I too die,
if we meet
as we were early promised
—*though I gave up*
*on promises long ago*—
if we meet, will you know me?

This person who carries
age and pain in her face,
whose black-winged hair
has turned the colour of your bones,
whose body has doubled,
will you know me?

And tell me,    tell me this,
are you free,
are you free from longing?

# Remembering Mary

*Mary Lonnberg Smith, 1939–1983*

I see you
standing on the summit
of some mountain,
notebook in hand, boot deep
in the wildflowers you so loved,
those swift sweet blooms that leave
in all too brief a season.
Your head is lifted as if listening,
mist hazes the still air between us
but you do not disappear.

# Flight in Autumn

*for C.B.G.*

"Look," you exclaimed, "Up there, the hawk,"
and pulled the car to one side, off the road.
Watching its long, slow circles
your face reflected pure delight
in that wild beauty, grace and power.

You did not know then, nor did we dream
that a dark bird of death had nested
deep within you, rested and grown
and spread its wide grey wings.
You did not know until its talons gripped
and the sharp beak began its cruel devouring.

Soon you will leave us, and that unfettered spirit
we so love in you will soar beyond our keeping.
But on a certain kind of windswept, golden day in autumn
we will be watching for a hawk, in graceful circling flight.

# Bridge on 219

Roar of the river
rushing below

blood throbs
pounds against her skull

spray swirling    spinning
the railing within reach

War in her head

# Suicide off Point Lobos

Only her small
young lungs rebel
Beneath the water's swell
sun glances off
last beads of breath
expelled
toward empty sky
Slack limbs submit
to pull of tide
Blank eyes
too long salt stung
stare into void
Deep thrum of silence
welcomed

# Limbo Again
*Venice, Italy*

Alone in this strange seaport,
this strange bed,
sleep comes slowly,
heavy and fitful,
dreams scattered as
friends and family.

I sink into a mirror
of remembered faces,
yearn for the soft cloth
of their known voices, cool
against the fever
of a nameless fear.
Hear only my heartbeat
clocking the distance between us.

Turning from the reflection
where change visits my face
I sense the time
when I will no longer be here
to see my children,
my children's children
in the fullness of their years.

Cracks open in the dense shell
that holds me. Quiet,
a stillness sometimes longed for
now terrifies as it engulfs.
Rising I unlock the casement;
torn by desire against desire
lean out with an old longing,
drawn to the sea's covetous lapping.

# Before the Snow

# Before the Snow
*Berkshire Mountains*

Here in deep woods
the early morning haze is damp
and redolent of pine.
Crows split the silence with
their graveled caws as crisp leaves
crackle underfoot like scolds
objecting to my presence. The grass
is white with frost, a veil tried on
before the heavy gown of winter.

I reach the pond where migrant geese
float wraithlike as they wait for
blanched late autumn sun
to burn away the mist. At last
it lifts, the long throats stretch,
harsh grating signals rasp the air.
And then, as one accord, a powerful
wild-winged thrash and flap
as they thrust skyward.

Earthbound, heart pounding,
each muscle straining up and up
I watch them disappear, compelled
like me toward distant golden light.

# Corcoran Lagoon
*Santa Cruz, California*

The breeze is pungent
with the scent of eucalyptus.
A crane perched on a floating log
preens with Edwardian elegance
oblivious to my presence.
The banks of the lagoon
are brushed with purple, pink,
pale yellow; reminders
that the seasons here
pass gently, announced by
certain flowering
or a subtle change of light.
Unlike that eastern shore
where more than fifty of my years
were weather sliced
precisely into quarters. Here
the illusion of unchanging pace
assures me there is endless time
stretched out and out. Grateful,
I allow myself this small deception.

# Anniversary
*for L.C.*

The milestone that loomed
shrinks
in the distance behind you
Your mother
thirty years gone
yet you still run in that race
her sweet breath
warm at your nape
and always
always the starter's gun
echoing the sound
of endings

# Dahomey Woman

*for L.C.*

Familiar shadows circle the floor,
death taps at your shoulder.
Burdened by love you dance faster,
move out of reach,
your reluctant skin
quivering beneath the hair shirt
you wear like a banner.

Life giver, lover of life,
what was bequeathed
and what taken?
The box that was willed you
fills over and over with stars.
Obedient to love you scatter them,
mark the way.

We who are still here
warm ourselves at your light
before we move out into darkness.

# Harvest

They wound around each other's lives,
tough, aging vines, choking all growth.
Old anger hung between them
purple as bruises, swollen as grapes.
Now, in the same ward where she died, he lies
bedridden, like some great behemoth decaying.

He curses his legs, those withered old
acquaintances who do not keep in touch.
Curses his quaking hands, the lifelong badges
of his calluses gone soft. Rails at the nurse
who cannot comprehend his foreign tongue.

Now when night terrors overwhelm
he calls for his children who no longer come.
Cries out their names, a litany of his failures;
forgetting years when their small hands
were picked away like burrs, their questions
answered with swift blows. When like their mother
they learned silence and retreat.

Grown children, who even now can hear the irritated
buzz of flies trapped at cracked windows, the scratch
and scurry of mice behind damp walls, where their
small clothes were hung on nails in worn apology.
Thin walls, through which the sounds they heard
were his coarse grunts, the whimpers
of the immigrant wife, only his body knew.

Night after night, throughout long days,
half-words, half-thoughts, fix in their arc, or fade.
He lies and listens for the sound of something turning,
stares at the ceiling toward vaster emptiness he fears.

# Caveat

The wind shrieks
shakes the house
between its teeth
No wings contest
the driven sky

Crouched underneath
the neighbor's eaves
a scrawny vagrant cat
usurps the Persian's shelter
licks at old scars
its mangy coat as grey
as this bleak morning

Catching my eye he arches
aims a harsh warning cry
in my direction
I draw the blinds
hunch shawled and shivering
by the hissing fire
the portents of this day
not in my favor

# Mirror

As a young girl
I made pomander balls
   as gifts
Thrust thorns of clove
into ripe globes of fruit
   hung them to dry
This morning I am reminded

# Secret from a Large Lady

Inside
no thin man
screaming to get out
Only
a young girl
head down
arms wound
around her knees
protected

# Behind the Walls

of the neat house
the groomed
and gardened house
behind the walls
sharp words
rip jagged wounds
across night air

Voices
bitter as bile
reiterate
old accusations
recriminations
venom
released
at short-changed life
disguised
behind largesse

Upstairs
the older children
make their own
compromise
One sits
headset plugged in
full volume
to a fast game
a furious game
of Nintendo

Door locked
the oldest
moves his world
to a safe
unsafe remove
with matches
glass pipe
small white crystals

In the basement
the playroom
the youngest one
the unexpected
the quiet one
jogs up and down
up and down

on outgrown
rocking horse
to the loud screech
the shrill screech
of worn-out springs
head muffled
in soft old
good old
safe old
blanky

# Trespass

Young sisters
little sisters
tall trees
cast shadows
dapple your thighs
your new breasts
as you dance

Smoke rises
from fires
in the camps
of the hunters
small pelts
stretched taut
scraped velvet
to touch

My sisters
little sisters
keep to the clearing
dance in close circle
joining your hands

# We Are Not the Enemy
*for Lu Chan Hall,*
*Lucille C., Maude M.*

We three
  are Black
  Chinese
  White

We three
  are mothers
  daughters
  grandmothers

We three
  enter any room
  take up space
  fill it

We three
  travel together
  heads turn
  eyes stare

We three
  know anger
  know sorrow
  embrace

We three
  climb over walls
  through cracks
  determined

We three
　　love life
　　love laughter
　　one another

We three
　　know who
　　know what
　　the enemy
　　　is

# Howling Coyote Writes
*Lucille*

I sent that card, the one
with the coyote baying at the moon,
the corny one that said,
"This is how I feel when I think about
how much I miss you," and then,
walking through Macy's
I spotted a big leather bag
just like the one you always carry
—the one with the clackety
wooden rings on the shoulder strap—
and knew I had to have it.

Now I carry it everywhere, heavy as absence.
The wooden rings clickety-clack as I walk
and it's your sound, and comforts me.
And when we talk on the phone and have to laugh
or cry over the screwy, scary world we live in,
that's when the word *friend* seems thinner
than bone soup when you are truly hungry,
and has to stretch to add the things
that sister, mother, daughter, can encompass.

So if in that small, southern place
two thousand miles away, you hear
a far-off howling, it's not the wind
or a stray cat, not even a coyote.
Only me, letting you know I'm trying hard
to fill the empty space where you should be.

# The Shearing

*for Li-Young Lee*

Today
when you appear
your visionary's brow
concealed
by a bandanna
I picture the shorn
dome beneath
envision
black silk strands
as they slipped
snake-like
to the floor
your
shaven skull
revealed.

Hair
its texture
taste
dark musky scent
is celebrated
all throughout your poems
it braids the lives
of those you love
with sensual tenderness
Beneath that scarf
it seems to me
a war is being waged

# The Great Escape
*Whatever happened to my old dancing shoes?*


You of the sixteen children, the tranquil brow,
and the serene demeanor, possessed of miraculous
insight and foresight, how did your daughter
spawn *this* daughter, famous for oversight
and as scattered as yesterday's family?
Oh, Grandmother, workmen traipse through my rooms,
I am surrounded by papers, long overdue,
plagued by the whine of my neighbor's power saw,
distracted by the clock's noisome tick,
measured and weighty as father's disapproval.

Harried by today, whelmed by tomorrow, I question
*whose* EYE peers down through that hole in the ozone.
I turn to I Ching only to find
that my fortune coins have absconded
and the tarot deck glued beyond redemption
with mint jelly from last week's rack of lamb.

Perhaps it is time to play loud music
I can dance to, though my neighbor
will stuff hairy knuckles into his ears
and mothers protest that their children
will awaken, forgetting they have long since
grown out of their jammies, into tuxedos
and wedding gowns, and Honda'd away.

I conjure magicians, escape artists, all wearing
the face of my favorite uncle. They whisk me
out of body, into a space as wide and peaceful
as Grandmother's lap. And I curl, lullabied,
cradled and rocked, naked and newborn, asking
no questions, needing no answers, no answers at all.

# Explorers

Here in this circle
of safety
we dare to risk
open in trust
break boundaries
of centuries
learn the rare joy
of being truly heard
Here in this circle
of unsafe women

# Workshop

Circular
currents
swirl
draw
scattered
fragments
Woman
connection
spinning
gathering
raw
nebulae
into
harmony

# Kayla

From the secret place
within
an amazing bird
takes wing
soars upward
seeking
light

# Paean

This is a poem for the woman
who said she was tired

This is a poem for the woman
who tired of running
backward and forward
till she wore a rut in the path
to her knees
This is a poem for the woman
who was tired of kneeling
who was tired of priests
and professors and panaceas
This is a poem for the woman
who was tired of being lied to
who was tired of lying to herself

This is a paean to the woman
who tired of being tired
Reclaimed herself

# The Passing

*Dorset, Vermont*

Light rain holds down the dust
of summer on the path,
quails scatter from tall marsh grass
as a brace of mallards chatter,
vexed at my intrusion.
At water's edge sleek minnows shiver
gleaming, and sounds of birds
and frogs and peepers
skim sweet air
like these long-winged
iridescent dragonflies,
or this ballet of skate bugs
whirling on the water's surface.
Around me myriad lives teem unaware
their numbers daily dwindle.
Young trees nearby wear rot
like feathers on the branch,
and some stand newly naked.
How did it come to this,
that you and I may be
among the last to know
this earth, this world
in all its innocent
and generous beauty.
How shall we ask forgiveness
for our desecration?

# Questions of War

# Some Things Never Change

*January 1991*

Today the Gulf War begins. Once again
I am reminded of notes I took at the zoo
in Buffalo, N.Y., during the Vietnam era.

They read,
> *Outside the Aviary Building is a huge cage.*
> *In it, solitary and brooding, a very large,*
> *powerful bird moves restlessly along a steel*
> *perch, gripping with talons capable of*
> *tearing a human to shreds.*

Attached to the cage is a placard,
> *The Bald Eagle is a predatory bird which exists*
> *by robbing the nests of smaller birds, and by*
> *preying on weak or wounded animals.*

Then adds,
> *The Bald Eagle is the symbol of our nation.*

Below that, a footnote,
> *The Bald Eagle is an endangered species.*

# Questions of War
*January 15, 1991*

I have seen my children as they came from me
squalling and kicking, the boys peeing in great arcs,
a daughter, crimson and mewling, each one
laid naked across my breast, the feral smell
of their birthing rising, my blood pasting their hair.
Nothing again will ever be so overwhelming,
nothing again so beautiful to see.

I watched a third son come into this world
perfect and whole, soon to be buried,
shut away in darkness. Another girlchild
born before her time and taken from me as I
listened to the cries of infants from the nursery,
milk gushing from me at the sound. *Dear God,
how precious, how irreplaceable is any life.*

I have known the joy of grandsons four times over,
each birth a miracle relived, each one so loved.
Yet there is fear and anger mixed with celebration;
the eldest of an age for war, the youngest, only
eight weeks on this earth. Eight weeks,
as we have been bombarded by the rhetoric of war,
the postured threats, the lessons of the past ignored
and all the children of the world in jeopardy.
How dare they ask us to yield up these innocents?

What if we all were willing to speak out, act out,
risk jail, or more than that, our lives
and not our children's to defy the madness?
The least, the very least we owe them is to know we tried.

# Documentary

*for Brian Willson, Holley, and Gabriel*


On the tracks
red flowers
the camera reeling
unreels
over and over

Seared
on the retina
the brain
the gut
the hearts refusal

The train
gathers speed
mouths open
in disbelief
the screams

The woman
whose mission is life
midwife
his wife
The young boy
the son
they watch this
we watch this

On the track
red blossoms
Anger
is the sieve
blood flows through

Violence
is a cold metal
iron train
steel tracks
wheels
relentless

The tall man
with no legs
speaks from his bed
speaks love
speaks peace

We are listening


*On September 21, 1987, Brian Willson, Vietnam veteran, was run down by a munitions train at the Concord Naval Station in a nonviolent protest against the shipping of arms to Central America, costing him both legs.*

# Letter to Dennis

I don't know if you remember me, it doesn't matter,
but I just read your piece in the *New Yorker*,
the one about your friend who's dying now of AIDS;
and for the first time I could cry the kind of tears
that come unbidden and unchecked, the way it happens
when you stand at that black wall in Washington, D.C.
and all the names stretch on forever,
thousands upon thousands, engraved like silent questions.

And when you lay your hand over a friend's name
or a stranger's, and it feels as cold as granite is,
or anybody's hand when they are dead,
and you stand asking *Why?* and there's no answer,
then nothing you can say or pray can seem to change that,
and you bottle up the part of you that thinks too much,
and feels too much, and asks too many questions.

I need to tell you that you helped the tears to come at last
for all the friends who've died these past few years.
Larry and Russell, Rick and Jim and Daniel, on and on
down the bleak line of those who've left us, willing or
unwilling, with calm acceptance, or in anger and despair.

The ache is still inside, but easier somehow because of you
and all who care enough to ease their passing
in homes or hospitals or hospices, those places where
the line is bottom, and the care is hands-on real.

And if there is a god whose eye is on the sparrow,
I'd like to ask that he or she would keep an eye on you
and others like you, in a world that most the time
seems blind and deaf and truly crazy. So thanks again,
your story is the kind of touchstone that we need
to keep us caring, keep us hoping, keep us sane.

# Letter from Sudan

He writes;
It is early, but already heat bakes the mind.
Here, near the railway station at Khartoum
the spectre of the massacre crouches like a shadow
over the streets of Ed Dueim.

The market is a silence of empty stalls.
In the square, small bowls at their feet,
spindly children wait in rows that stretch further
than the mind can tolerate. The harsh fist of hunger
has sunk hollows below their eyes and dulled their minds.
Between their lines men in long white *jhallabias*
stalk stiff-legged, sharp-eyed as birds of prey.

Nothing flourishes here but the black market;
only the vultures, the merchants and militia are sated.
Soon the vendors will arrive in eddies of dust and noise
and some of the bowls will be filled, at least for the moment,
as even these scrawny waifs are useful for exchange.

As I read, the shadow hovers over this far-off house,
descends over the crimsoned square in China, over
the hovels of Soweto, the dwellings of all the oppressed
where women hide in fear and weep over their children.
The walls of this room swell with dark whispers.
Spells swarm in the air around me like hornets before the sting.

# Mollie's Restaurant

*a true story*


Early morning
passing through Livermore
I stop at a coffee shop
the only place that's open

Head for the rest room
two signs
Stallions
Nags

I find a booth
sit down
check the menu
order
sit back
look around

High up
hung on four walls
count
84 rifles / shotguns
29 handguns / assorted
15 sabers

From the ceiling
too numerous to count
miscellaneous
antique guns
scimitars
machetes
daggers
stilettos
etcetera

and
perhaps unintentionally
subconsciously
metaphorically
a boomerang

On the exit door
close by
a bulletin
advertising gun sales
shooting meets

Below that
a big sign

Guns Can't Walk
Guns Can't Talk
Guns Don't Kill
Bad People Kill People
Outlaws Love Gun Laws

Waiting for coffee
head buried
in the paper
I read

"Boy Nine Kills Playmate
Accidentally
With Father's Loaded Gun"

Quietly
carefully
creasing the paper
I tear the headline out

Get up
amble over
real casual
steal a tack from the bulletin
add the headline to the sign

Walk out
feeling some better
Not much

# San Joaquin

Grapes grow thick on the vines
in the San Joaquin Valley
the rich fertile valley
where young children harvest

Fruits of their labours
are the dark grapes of cancer
that cluster on delicate
vines of their veins

Scarred hands catch the sobs
from mouths of the mourners
knot in clenched fists
as small coffins are lowered

Families stand stunned
bewildered at gravesides
gather to them the children
who somehow survive

They too have no future
but the fields and the baskets
the sour sick breath
of disease in their lungs

And here in the valley
as green as the money
the pittance that's paid them
they must remain silent

*No hablan inglés*
*no tienen dinero*
*no tienen futuro*
*no hay manera de quejarse*

The long ear of the *Migra*
listens for voices
bold voices that dare
to speak out the truth

While the San Joaquin Valley
grows ever more fertile
on the bodies of children
who nourish the soil
the sweet bodies of babies
that nourish the soil

# San Joaquín

Las uvas crecen grandes en las vides
del Valle de San Joaquín
el rico y fértil valle
donde pequeños niños cosechan

Los frutos de sus labores
son las oscuras uvas cancerosas
que se amontonan en las delicadas
ramas de sus venas

Manos cicatrizadas recojen el llanto
de las bocas de los deudos
para volverse luego puños
cuando bajan los pequeños ataúdes

Las familias paradas se quedan
sin entender ante las tumbas
que reúnen a los niños
que de alguna forma sobreviven

Ellos también no tienen futuro
sino campos y canastas
el aliento amargo y dañino
de la enfermedad de sus pulmones

Y aquí en el valle
tan verde como el dinero
lo poco que les pagaron
ellos deben quedarse callados

No hablan inglés
no tienen dinero
no tienen futuro
no hay manera de quejarse

La larga oreja de la Migra
anda buscando voces
voces desafiantes que se atrevan
a proclamar la verdad

Mientras el Valle de San Joaquín
crece cada vez más fértil
gracias a los cuerpos de los niños
que nutren los campos
los dulces cuerpos de bebés
que nutren los campos

*Translation by Francisco X. Alarcón*

# Prayer to the Ancestors
*Ohlone Indian Burial Ground*

Your children come to you
We come to ask you
to awaken the ancient wisdom
that rests with you
the ancient wisdom
that sleeps in us

Let your spirit blow
through the sacred flutes
that are your bones

We will listen
We will listen for you
in the running waters
in the call of birds
in the night sounds

Send to your children
the words of your wisdom
that we may heal greed
heal anger
That we may bring peace .
to the earth our mother
peace to one another

That we may know
that peace begins
in our hearts

Send to your children
the words of your wisdom
that we may hear them
that we may speak them

That we may not be silenced

# Why This Is Not a Poem

The photographs begin innocently, innocuously enough. In a cantina a nervous bride and groom embrace for the camera, a small child balances on his proud young father's hands, an old man brooms coffee beans under a tropic sun.

Slowly, subtly the mood changes. A photograph of a bar, empty, except for a man seated below three large posters. A holy scene of the nativity, a jolly gringo Santa, an Anglo woman, her blonde hair barely veiling large breasts, her hand posed suggestively between spread thighs.

On the following page, a stark photo of a group of small children gathered with closed, enigmatic faces, staring at a Rorschach of fresh blood. A student's blood, spilled on the cracked concrete of a public street. It is El Salvador, not Alabama or Ohio, but déjà vu rises with my gorge.

I study a scene depicting women marching defiantly before a government building banging skillets with forks and spoons. They wear on their heads white scarves embroidered with the names of *los desaparecidos,* sons and daughters who have disappeared without a trace. These women are aware of what they risk in their protest. Know they may find imprinted on their doors the warning mark of *Mano Blanca,* the White Hand, signature of the Death Squad. My thoughts rush to my own sons, my daughter, her sons. I become the woman who wears the scarf, my children's names embroidered in red silk, red letters that drip blood, drip tears.

I become the young woman who writes in white paint on the glass window of a coffin, and I translate in my poor Spanish, *Te amo, jamas te olvido le contere a mi hija de ti quando créce y pueda entendere.* "I love you, I will never forget you. I will tell my daughter about you when she grows up." I stare at the face through the glass lid, through the painted words. A face so searingly beautiful in death, I cannot tell if it is a boy or girl. Only that it is too young.

I dream again that night of Rosario Godoy de Cuevas, whose husband Carlos was abducted, reported stuffed into the trunk of a car by men in uniform as he was returning home. It is 1984. The place is Guatemala, not El Salvador. But like the wives, mothers, lovers, and children of El Salvador and Chile, Rosario searches the morgues, the dumps, the newspapers, the secret death lists, for some sign, any sign, of the loved one.

She does this for two years. She is *Rosario*, who dares to protest in public the assassination of Cardinal Rivera. *Rosario*, mother of Augusto Rafael, born after his father's disappearance. *Rosario*, who, with her brother and her son, is found in a car at the bottom of a steep canyon. An accident, according to the scant newspaper report. When relatives recover the bodies it is discovered that the nails had been torn from her child's small fingers.

I awaken to her screams. They are my own. Screams that pierce like the knives used to mutilate, to torture, to kill the ones who have dared to disagree with those in power, the ones seeking power.

Guatemala, El Salvador, Chile. The list grows. Always we ask, did no one smell the stink from the furnaces of Belsen, Dachau? Hear the cries from Treblinka? Was it so long ago that we have forgotten? Do we heed the voices of South Africa, Harlem, Big Mountain? Native Americans forced from the reservations they were once herded into. Mexicans turned back from the land taken from them by our military. Everywhere, voices silenced or ignored. I struggle with my anger.

I receive a phone call from Nicaragua. It becomes evident that the call is being monitored. I am told that when certain key words are spoken a computer automatically clicks into the line, yet accept this possibility, this probability, with no surprise. We still live in a country where I may read these words aloud, yet the free world shrinks as the voices of intimidation grow louder.

At a workshop Forché admonishes, "When writing political poetry, allow the readers to make their own connections. Leave out how the readers should feel. Don't preach or urge to action." *Mea culpa*, I am guilty of these things.

That is why this is not a poem. Why the feelings I am expressing are still too overwhelming to be neatly distilled. But when the poem is written, it will remind us, when each of us dies and sinks into the brown, the red, the yellow ochre of our sick mother earth, when she trembles in her last throes, all our still bones, white gleaming, will weave their spare symmetry at last, into belated integration. And if we wait in silence till that time, the only echo that we hear will say, *"Too late, too late . . ."*

*The photographs referred to are from* El Salvador, *by Carolyn Forché. Harry Mattison, Susan Meiselas, and Fae Rubenstein, editors. Writers and Readers Publishing Cooperative: New York and London, 1983.*

# Washing the Stones

## For Acer

*see where he moves*
*he leaves a wake of tears*
*see in the path of his going*
*the banners of regret*

*see just above him the cloud*
*of welcome     see him rise*
*see him enter the company*
*of husbands     fathers     sons*

—*Lucille Clifton*
The Book of Light

# FOR ACER and all the years

*White of snow*
*White of torn ribbons*
*White of the starburst in our bed*

Who can remember our pale young faces
as we ran toward the dark space
unafraid     Bold then, or foolish
when rent was a thing to worry     Threadbare
and the meat reserved for the child

Who else will remember the cribs we leaned into
our hands lifting another, another,
and another child, and the crying ceased
Magic we were, and the magic in hands
heating the damp of hidden places     The coming together
of bodies     White of the starburst in our bed

Our terror in parting in times of war
or the deaths tearing our lives
The bearing up of our fear
like a chalice cupping the wine, the unholy dreams
drenched as they came to being

The white petals of snow wilting
on new turned earth     A grave
and a mockery of roses dropping with the soft thud
of footsteps on a small white box
The helpless gestures of hands

And who will remember the loss of innocence
trailing torn white ribbons of light
knotting the spaces between us     Who then
but you and I, our mouths swollen with love, or pain
our hands outstretched as we turn again to each other

*The chalice brimming*
*The dark space looming*
*The starburst warming our bed*

# Long Run Play
*for my husband*

Amateurs
we opened
without rehearsal
without repertoire
to mixed reviews
Learned
to revise the script
to play
with or without
supporting cast

Our dialogue costumes
have altered
The scenery shifts
time passes
our technique improves
We now use
a minimum of props
dispense
with makeup masks
and stand-ins
No longer vie for billing

# Response

Uneasy
drifting in and out
of slanted dreams
I move
to lie against you
seeking comfort
Even in sleep
you are attuned
sense subtle difference
in my touch
You turn and hold me
body spooned to mine
Rising    falling
against my hair
your breath lulls
by its rhythm
Cradled in warmth
I am sustained
aware of tenderness
that in this moment
of my need is dearer far
than your quick passion

# List

How can I go to market
this spring day
move under stark fluorescence
behind a basket made of steel.

Nearing the acacia
I fall captive
held by its languorous rich smell.

I press against rough bark
breasts aching
thighs wet with my own sap

Nowhere does my list say
make love
under an acacia tree
at noon

# Adventuress

From our warm bed
hearing the ebb and surge
of waves, I see myself
adrift but unafraid
on some uncharted sea.
Yes, I am brave,
meanwhile aware
of harbor and anchor
lying next to me.

# Short Poem for Acer, Sleeping

Your head pokes
from a cocoon
of tangled sheets
Your feet
splay out the other end
like long white rabbit ears
All you are wearing
is an anxious frown
I'm not used to seeing you
so vulnerable
Want to cover you
with my body

# Of Dreams, Nightmares, Osmosis

Your foot jerks, erratic, against mine.
Blindly you swat at cold night air, legs thrashing.
I stroke you, murmuring, *It's all right, it's all right,*
a litany, over and over until you sink back into calm,
deep sleep, and I once more begin the slide
into that world where we may travel, yet have no control.

The still life of the interior stirs, squirms,
furtive as unseen larvae hatching in the wool.
Broken threads wind, drawing me down a deserted road
where there are signs of struggle, but no sign of life.

Suddenly you are running toward me, carrying
a gift tied with ribbons curling back to our childhood.
The dream loses shape, light pries at my eyelids,
they open to the moon, huge white enigma at our window.

In the morning you tell me of your nightmare, of being
lost in darkness, hearing the sickening hiss and suck
of plunging blade, raw scrape of steel on bone.
How you ran wet with the sweat of fear on twisted,
unfamiliar roads,    and turning to look behind you
saw coarse threads,    moving,    floating toward you,
weaving themselves into soft ribbons,    whispering
my presence near you in newly light, bright air.

# Fusion

I see your features
mirrored
in our children
Scattered at random
among grandchildren
like gifts
or prizes won

I watch them
remembering
your adolescence
your young manhood
Find
I cannot recall
a world
before I knew you
or imagine
a world without you
and I hold you
closer    closer

# Choice

Blindfolded
I would know
the touch
the taste
the smell of you
among a thousand others
and knowing, choose you

# On Second Thought

*Last night's inspiration: write an erotic poem*

Now I sit here
cold early morning light
hard chair

Your body, familiar as my own
passes the window
working the garden
in sweaty
earth stained garb
old flop-brimmed hat

You are no help
conjure no visions
of flame-tongued nights
mad paroxysms of lust
or Sutrian delights

Right now a second cup of coffee
a ripe and succulent peach
tempt me to leave this task
luring my sense with a pull
stronger than your proximity

Perhaps this is all
that need be said
If you came in, touched me
took me to our bed
my breasts would swell
my nipples rise as they do now

To hell with peaches
there is sweeter juice
let someone else write poems
Come in
there's better planting to be done

# Greedy

Oh smarmy treacly
June moon schmaltz of it
The triple sundae
topped with everything
The hot plum pudding
brandied sauce of it
The soft fuzz on your belly
and ah    those bony knees
and oh    that mouth
and yes    oh yes
this making love
the lick and tongue of it

# Careful What You Wish For

A shawl of rain wraps the fall landscape,
leaches the early morning light
that shrouds Mt. Greylock and the valley floor.
From the front door I see the pond
where three white geese bob imperturbable as nuns,
their long necks question marks
against wind-ruffled water.

I cannot settle. Invent more reasons
not to sit down at my desk. Avoid my workroom,
that cul-de-sac of good intentions, and everywhere
excuses, a reproach of dishes, unmade bed, a place
for everything and nothing in its place, including me.

I have been here for just one week, and now
this longed for solitude, this ideal time and space
in which to work, lose magic in the face of separation.
I prowl from room to room, grow edgy, wait for the phone
to ring. Cross on the calendar the weeks till your arrival.

# First Things First
*Dorset, Vermont*

It's Sunday, and the carillon of the white-steepled
church across the way chimes sweetly in spiced air
that bears the scent of frost and wood smoke.
Missing your warmth I start a fire in the woodstove
for here    in this New England fall
the air is crisp as the first bite of apple.

Last night I watched in awe as wild geese flew
in silhouette across the sunset's wild extravaganza
filling the air with their unearthly cries
until the moon carved its curved scimitar
across night sky. This morning, against amazing blue,
clouds scud their sails before high winds
that rustle leaves of russet, gold, vermilion,
transcending all clichés of autumn brilliance.

It's difficult to picture you in Indonesia
surrounded by exotic sights and sounds,
moving through sweltering air that bears the peal
of temple bells, the pungent scent of incense.
Once more we've traveled in our disparate ways
and must bridge half a world to meet, but suddenly
that time seems infinitely far away. I try to call
but lines refuse to braid our separate worlds,
a nervous crackle of wire steals your voice
and there is only empty air between us.

Dear love, adventure's sweet, but I'm reminded
of that admonition, *Time's a commodity, on which
alas, there is no guarantee.* So, barring fate,
soon we will meet with much to tell,    and time
to share the telling. But first, before one treasure
is unwrapped, one story told,    one thing unpacked,
yes first, be silent with your mouth on mine,    and hold me.

# Ceremony

Muted
insistent
this soft
    subtle music surrounds me
    as warm scented water
    flows over and around me

*like music*
*like silk*

Fragrant
and silken
my robe
    will flow from me
    as you will surround me
    insistent yet subtle

*as music*
*as silk*

# Companion of My Heart of My Life

If touch was once the drowning ecstasy
and the hollow of your throat
a valley for exploration
If the consuming passion devoured us
and your body loomed as a mountain
one climbed again and again
to relive the wild exhilaration
then understand that now
the deepening lines of your face
the shadows that bruise the skin
years of slow changes
so subtle that they catch the heart
on sudden recognition
arouse in me a tenderness that has no equal
The fire that leapt and flickered wildly
burns surely    sweetly    steady now    as truth

# Compañero de mi Corazon de mi Vida

Si el tocarte era una vez la ectasia ahogante
y el hueco de tu cuello
un valle que explorar
Si la pasión consumidora nos devorara
y tu cuerpo surgiera como una montaña
que escalara una y otra vez
para revivir la loca alegría
entonces comprende que ahora
las lineas que se profundizan en tu rostro
las sombras que magullan tu piel
años de cambios lentos
tan sutiles que en reconocimiento repentino
sorprenden al corazón
despiertan en mi una ternura sin igual
el fuego que brotaba y vacilaba con frenesi
sin duda arde dulce    ahora firme    como verdad

*Translation by Elba Sanchez*

# In Time of War

*for Donna and her father, Ace, circa 1954*

You came to us in the postwar year,
in the wake of your unnamed sister's loss.
All of the promised miracles were ours,
your every move amazing. We were heady
with welcome, overwhelmed with joy.

Almost six years went by before your
brothers swam into the bottomless pool
that was our love. Almost eight years
before your father was called again to war.

Dressed like a stranger in his somber uniform
a small launch carried him to a destroyer
shrouded in heavy fog offshore.
Shivering in cold dawn I watched him vanish,
the pale moon of his oval face, white cap
and lifted palm all disappearing into mist.

You, my small daughter, were my link with
distant home, in that strange Navy town.
And when each morning you rode off to school,
shoes shined, dress pressed and spotless,
homework so carefully prepared, I ached
to see you leave, and my long days
hung on the hook of your return.

The first thing you would ask
was if there was a letter, and in each one
he'd write, *I know you'll do your best*
*at school and help your mom. Be a good girl,*
*and keep a good watch on your brothers.*

And oh   you were,   you did,   and when
you bent to them the thick braids
fell like weights on narrow shoulders
and your dark eyes were as serious as parsons'.

Each night you showed the boys his picture.
They kissed it as you did, and when he finally returned
how sad you were at bedtime as they backed away
from this intruder, and kissed his photograph instead.

Do you remember how you waited with me
on the crowded dock and watched his ship
grow from a tiny blip on the horizon
till it loomed above us? How still you were
through the long hours it took. And it was then
I realized your months of extra good behavior
were insurance you were paying on his safe return.

Now you are grown, the same thick hair, wide eyes,
sons of your own who tower over you. I see you
watch your father age, knowing there are no rites,
no incantations, no insurance that will keep him safe
or with you always, and I take his picture.

# Poem for Acer
*Valentine's Day, February 14, 1992*

Something a grandson said today
took me away from California
and this redwood deck
to the first place
we lived as newlyweds,
that now passé expression

But that is what we were,
old-timey innocents, amazed
at the long wished-for gift
of waking in one another's arms

I still recall each room
of that old brownstone,
chairs borrowed,
curtains cut from bedspreads,
even strange smells that wafted
through the air shaft
in that closet of a kitchen
on West 56th Street

On Sunday mornings we would
stroll in Central Park,
and afterward you'd lie
flat-bellied on the floor
before the fire
and read the *Times*
while I fixed brunch

Evenings, after you studied
we read aloud to one another
and almost every night and twice on Sundays
we made love, made love

Then for the first time you were off to war
and life, real life, began in earnest.
Well, that was 1943, and this is 1992, and we
to our surprise, are white-haired,
full of history, a little wisdom,
three thousand miles from our beginnings,
closer to endings than seems possible

Dear love, the years have telescoped
to take us by surprise
Sometimes I see our life together
pass before me in the way
they say it does before you drown,
and then I surface, grateful
for past and present precious time
we now count day by day

# Wrong Journey
*May 21, 1992*

Here is the suitcase
packed for the trip
not taken
This is not
the planned holiday
but an unholy day
Here is his wife
gripped in the arms
of their children
all of their lives
imploding
Here are the stunned faces
the animal sounds
The news falls like a club
indifferent club
of the slaughterhouse
no warning

# For This Journey

We are not supposed to be here
where they speak only euphemese,
here in this room of stainless sinks,
strange instruments and acrid chemicals
for preservation,    but have persuaded them
to let this husband,    father,    lover,    dear companion
be bathed and dressed by known,    loved hands.

We are not prepared,    who could be,    for this,
this silent stranger, sheet draped,
refrigerator cold, skin mottled bluish grey.
*I warm your face between my hands,    your lips with mine.*
*Folds of your neck are pink, soft, partly thawed.*
*Their living texture shocks.    I know this skin,*
*these folds,    stroke them,    shut out the room,    pretend.*

You are made ready as you would have wished.
A favorite sweatshirt, worn khakis,
two-for-one-price sneaks (you called them "spiffy")
and in your hands the battered, stained safari hat
that traveled with you on each new adventure.

We drape the muted fabric of your Balinese sarong
over the satin lining of the coffin,
surround your stillness with mementos, smile, weep,
at shared stories of your well-lived, well-loved life,
strew petals on the strong and perfect body
that hid its fatal flaw from you,    from us.

Now it is time. We gather round this man,
the hub of all our lives. Hands joined, we sing,
speak final words. Leave with a last caress.
Now he is ready for this journey.    We are not.

# Novitiate

*...the walk through the widow's door*
*is a long walk. —Lucille Clifton*

Inside the shower
cold tile
becomes a wailing wall
Grief
batters against it

Nothing cracks
nothing breaks
nothing changes

No one to hear
curse     pleas
wild ragged keening
No one to stop her fists
that beat
against this silence

Her world
blurs
in thick steam
dissolves
beneath the scalding
rush of water
against
resistant skin

Scrubbed clean and pale
contained
as any nun
she opens the door
to the long hall
walks slowly through
wrapped in his robe
ill-fitting
dark new habit.

# Third Person Singular

Words thicken on her tongue
or will not come at all
Sleepless at night
sleepwalking numb
through days that
bend beneath
a grief so vast
her whole world
tilts

In a strange way detached
she is both watcher
and the watched
who waits to see
if she decides
it would be easier
to ride this slant
straight down
and off

# death rattle

look
look under that rock
look closer
beneath its shadow

eyes hooded
the split-tongue darting
the exquisite
patterned back
the pale cold belly
concealed

I know this snake
I have walked this path before
wary
of going around the bend

# As the Thread Unravels

There is a woman in this room
who is mourning
She is rocking back and forth
She is rocking and weeping
She is a woman rocking the world
A woman rocking herself
There is a woman in this room
making sounds of an animal
A woman in this room whose rage
runs as deep as her fear and her sorrow
A woman whose rage and whose fear and whose sorrow
threaten to engulf her
In this room is a woman who is reaching her limit
A woman who denied there were limits
who trusted   who fought   who could not utter the word   *helpless*
In this room is a woman clinging by a thread to reason
Clinging to a thread with her right hand
as the left one fumbles for scissors

# intruder

there's something set loose in my house
it shrinks     skitters beneath baseboards
across the sink
peers up from the dark drain

sometimes it swells so huge
its sigh sucks the air

i can't breathe

there it is     don't you see it
see its scrabbling prickly legs
scuttle across my pillow
scurry up the wall

sometimes it waits over my bed
hangs on strange twisted thread

is it strands of my hair

there     hear the click of its frantic busy claws
see it grin     See its little hooked teeth

# forewarning

a wet snout
roots
through my dreams
split hoofs
paw for droppings
that escape
the light of day
now I peer
into   faces   mirrors
alert
for raw muzzles
dirt beneath the nails

# Bête Noire

How do I write
of nights
spent reading
until the words run
all together and away
as if to say, *Enough,*
and the book drops
unnoticed from my hand?

Or watching images
that jabber on a screen
having no more to say
to me, than I to them,
until at last
both ears and eyes rebel
and send me from my chair
to our old bed
once dearly shared.

No matter what the hour,
how deep this aching need
for sleep, how many
cups of broth, warm milk,
or sedatives I take,
I'm wide awake the moment
that our mattress sighs
beneath this single weight,
and once again the mind begins
its endless spin, circling
relentless, partnerless,
on the dark dance floor of the night.

# Aftermath

In early years
they told me
knowledge
was strength
was what
I would need
to survive

I believed
wanted to know
everything

Now the mind
longs
to turn back
empty itself
Wishes
the brain
to be a new
smooth egg
unbroken

# Kid Love

A week or so after the funeral
my niece Kate called, and I told her,
Kate, you know, I can't eat anything but
white food. Mashed potatoes, noodles,
Cream of Wheat, bimbo bread. *Yeah,*
she said, *I do know. Me too. Me,*
*the live-right health-food maven.*

Then she told me that the other day, Budi,
he's eleven, said, *Kate*—he calls her Kate
like my kids call me Maudie—*Kate,* he says,
*I can't believe you're eating that junk stuff.*
And she answered, *Kid food, Budi. Right now*
*I need this kid food; you know, comfort stuff.*

Next day he came home from school,
walked past Kate, real cool,
mumbled, *swapped my lunch,*
and dropped a Hostess Twinkie on the table.

# The Balance Game

I'm wearing the maroon nighty that I loved, you hated.
Not that I sleep any better, but it wraps around me softly.
Oh, and the kids gave me a microwave so now I seldom cook.
Eat when, what and if I want to, and
I don't miss doing all that laundry.

I sold your old car *and* mine. The new one's automatic,
air-conditioned, has shocks, springs, an airbag too.
Even the garage door is automatic now, and the lawn has
a real sprinkler system that got rid of all those gophers.

You'd be surprised, and pleased I think,
to know I did our taxes, even took care
of all the paper legalese that swamped me
those first months while still in shock
and wondering how to make it through the day.

And even though they're hurting, our kids are so darn
caring, they call and come around. I'm grateful.
Sometimes I wonder if you know we have another grandchild
on the way, and how strange it seems that he won't know you.

The widow word. I still can't make it fit. For fifty-seven
years since we were kids we shared our lives, so now it seems
impossible that you are gone. I see you everywhere,
and there are times I still forget and think you're here.

You know, for months I couldn't write at all, then suddenly
the words about your death began to pour. Now I feel free
to write at any time of day or night without the fear
that I might wake you.    Oh, that I could.

# Wharf to Wharf
*Santa Cruz, California*


Today
in heavy early morning mist
tasting of brine
our sons ran in the race
from wharf to wharf
along the oceanfront
a race you ran beside them
in years past
Later
they placed their numbers
weighted with stones
on your new grave
And I
whose life was paced
alongside yours
since childhood
fall behind
now wearing numbers
I cannot decipher
borne on salt-bitter currents
in your long shadow's wake

# Marking Your Absence

The first frost
dulls late autumn's fire
A blaze of leaf
becomes
brown tattered tracery
on frozen ground

The precise moment
of transition escapes
Perceptions heighten
beyond bearing
Your absence
more tangible than my presence

# Rebirth

*Smooth,* he said
*your belly, breasts*
*so smooth*
his gone voice
suddenly alive

I wake to urgent hunger
at bay these nine months
since his death
Painful this birth
after the barren interval
Nothing to hold
but this dense weight
of absence

# Treading New Water

The lake was smooth, flat,
wider than vision,
the water sun-gilded,
bathed in the meaning of tranquil.

I swam next to, around
the dory where you lazed,
then, with long, easy
strokes, ventured further.

After a patient while
you signaled it was time
for moving on,
I shook my head, gestured

that I was turning back to harbor,
the nearby dock and pebbled beach.
Smiling, you waved good-bye,
lifted the heavy oars and turned away.

Swift, smooth as seal I dove,
then suddenly exhausted, surfaced
treading chilled, choppy water
beneath a swiftly darkening sky.

Calling your name I searched
the blank horizon as it faded,
saw the familiar shoreline vanish,
awakened shivering, in our newly outsize bed.

# Small Things

A friend called early,
hoarse-voiced from lack of sleep
to read his newborn poem
about the woman who'd said good-bye.
How it felt, discovering
small things she'd left behind.
A faded blouse, a scarf,
the lingering odor of her sex
as he lay resting
in their bed last night.

After his call, half-buried
memories rush back
too vivid, too alive,
of how someone,
I can't remember who,
brought me the clothing
you were wearing
at the moment of your death.

How I turned and pressed my face
—it's what you do—
into that bundle of no-moreness,
startled by pungent dampness,
your slacks, sodden with urine
lost in that last moment's shock.

Then later, disentangling your shirt
to launder for a son, a grandson,
or a friend who might find comfort
wearing the last thing close to you,
discovered the jagged tear
ripped by strange hands
that laboured frantically
to bring you back.

Such simple things
a scarf,   a scent,   a shirt,
to open wounds that spill
not blood,   but poems.

# Imperfect Silence

*We have been exiled from silence.*
—Li-Young Lee

Street sounds sift through
the rustle of dry leaves,
blend with the buzz
and hum of a computer,
reminding me that yesterday

a woman, deaf from childhood
signed with quick hands
to say there is a difference
in interior shades of silence;
for instance when she is immersed
in deep or shallow water

Another, blind from birth,
says there are certain sounds
that splash her world
with colours she can see
but cannot name

Lately I read that infants
floating like lazy fish in
utero, hear and remember
certain voices after birth

Then what of after death?
Will we know perfect silence
as is claimed? And if so,
how perfect is that silence
when no song of bird,
no sound of children,
no familiar voice
or love cries filter through?

# Second Spring
*Elegy, California, 1994*


This spring the colours pierce,
too opulent, too vivid.
If I must deal again with flowers
let them be small and unassuming.

Something bruised in me
longs for gardens of my childhood
where no bird of paradise took root
shrilling purple and orange,
beside camellias, acid pink,
vaunting their fullness.

Havens, where no calla lilies flourished
amid a passion of bougainvillea,
or serpent stems of orchids coiled
beneath exotic, unfamiliar trees
bursting with garish blossoms.

And the hyacinths. If you only knew
how the heavy smell
of these thick clustered bells,
once sweetly sensual, now sickens.

Here in this cemetery these gaudy
crimson tulips assault, alongside
florid jonquils whose cruel mouths
trumpet false promise of rebirth.

*Look into my eyes, are there reflections? Close them.*
*Close my ears against this noisome brilliance.*

# The Other Side

*Response to Lynda Barry*

*She said she crossed*
*over the mountain*
*to the other side*

*and stood*
*in an ocean of marigolds*
*She said they were beautiful*

*that the people*
*who tend them*
*told her the flower*
*was their telephone*
*that never broke down*

*She said*
*she thought it was me*
*they were calling*
*that they miss me*
*dream about me*
*send their love*
*sweet kisses*

Hello      Hello

I keep calling
I can hear
a little hum
but no voices

I love you
Where are you
are you       are you

Every day I climb
as high as I can
and look over the edge

Is it Spring
on the other side
Is it Summer

Here
all the marigolds
are brown and frozen

# Wishbones

Save wishbones
paint them golden
place between settings
at the holiday table
let all who have gathered
make extravagant wishes
they would never reveal

Take wishbones
paint them silver
share them with children
trusting small children
who have faith in their wishes
in secret dream wishes
where magic is real

Old wishbones
paint them tear-stained
take them down to the grave site
lift the moss    lift it gently
then bury the bones

Bury the bones
with impossible wishes
though all have been broken
ask for a sign

# Washing the Stones

Armed with buckets
and small brushes, two grandsons
four and six, trudge beside me
to the family plot. Their faces serious,
pleased to be included in this ritual,
the washing of the stones.

Scrubbing at leaf-gummed
residue of winter, we speak of the
grandfather they dimly recollect.
And then because they know
all creatures die when they are old,
ask where *my* stone will be,
assure me earnestly that they
will clean mine too.     *We know how,*
the youngest says, and     *Look,*
*we're really good at it.*
Questions follow about burial
and death, but before long,
their interest turns to small boy
talk, their treble voices
livening this resting place.

Above the site a canopy of trees
displays tight buds, soon to unfurl
just as these sturdy blood-kin boys
are opening,     as side by side
with care we wash the stones.

# A Chorus of Doves

This morning I was awakened
by a rooster's crow. I don't know
what he was doing at that ungodly hour
here by the ocean, instead of on
a fence post on some farm.
But there was something thin and lonely
in his cry. Not like the mourning doves who
gathered, perched on our back porch railing
after our sweet baby died,
as if to let us know all other soft, small
creatures mourned. Their gentle mama-coo sound
rising,    falling,    filling the too empty air.

Since you died, leaving us all
without a last good-bye, I've thought a lot about
the question of an afterlife, the spirit world,
the soul world really. I'm uncertain of
the difference, though there seems to be one.
Right now, most everything's uncertain
and I neither doubt, believe, nor can rely
on anything, the ground so shifty underfoot.

I have strange thoughts, like wondering if that
rooster could be my father, who never could abide
to see me cry. He died still crowing at age
eighty-nine, perhaps come back at this cruel time
to let me know he's sorry, for having been
the puffed up banty cock he was in life.

Or was it you, remembering how years ago
the pain of that hard morning eased for me, hearing
that haunting chorus of grey doves? You never could
sing much,   still,   it would be like you to try.
Embarrassed by all the fuss your dying caused,
but sort of liking it—everyone crying,
missing you, talking you up. Something you wouldn't
have put up with for a minute, in *this* life.

But it was probably just some old rooster,
lost and pitiful, doing what roosters do
when there's no hen around for comfort.

I guess we're all a little lost, crying, crowing,
whatever gets us by, until the hard-as-stone ache
eases. And after a long while, you start to think
a time could come when one might even try to sing,
a little tremulous at first, maybe a soft, dove cry.

# Coin of This Realm

This is not despair,
not the retreat into the deep wound
but a conscious living of each day

This is the placing of one foot before the other,
not the free stride of the unencumbered
but the careful tread of the initiated foot

This is learning how to walk
without familiar landmarks, alone
even in the company of others,
not ready yet for new direction

This is the living of each day, aware
that what you cannot predict
may still loose sudden tears, yet
that laughter too is possible

This is when you struggle
as plants in arid soil
strive without conscious knowing
to stay alive until the rain

This is a time for faith
that this most naked agony of loss
will ease, and not corrode the spirit

This is the time to trust that day after
laboured day you will move forward,
open to joy as well as pain;
two-sided coin, you proffer for remembrance

# About the Author

MAUDE MEEHAN, a native New Yorker, is a poet, editor, lecturer, and lifelong activist. She began writing poetry at age fifty-five, soon after moving to California. She has since published two poetry collections, *Chipping Bone* (Embers Press, 1985) and *Before the Snow* (Moving Parts Press, 1991). Her work has appeared in many journals and in numerous anthologies, including *Lovers* (Crossing Press, 1989) and *The Tie That Binds* (Papier-Mache Press, 1992), and she has edited and coedited several anthologies, including *Moonjuice I–IV.* She has also coauthored a film script, *Wheels of Summer,* with Dan Bessie. She has a daughter, two sons, five grandsons, and one great-grandson. Widowed after fifty-seven years with her life partner, "Acer," she resides in Santa Cruz, California, where she teaches creative writing and is currently working on her second film script.

# Papier-Mache Press

At Papier-Mache Press, it is our goal to identify and successfully present important social issues through enduring works of beauty, grace, and strength. Through our work we hope to encourage empathy and respect among diverse communities, creating a bridge of understanding between the mainstream audience and those who might not otherwise be heard.

We appreciate you, our customer, and strive to earn your continued support. We also value the role of the bookseller in achieving our goals. We are especially grateful to the many independent booksellers whose presence ensures a continuing diversity of opinion, information, and literature in our communities. We encourage you to support these bookstores with your patronage.

We publish many fine books about women's experiences. We also produce lovely posters and T-shirts that complement our anthologies. Please ask your local bookstore which Papier-Mache items they carry. To receive our complete catalog, send your request to Papier-Mache Press, 135 Aviation Way, #14, Watsonville, CA 95076, or call our toll-free number, 800-927-5913.